MARCO 🌐 POLO

D0355962

er

Tips

PARIS

GREAT BELGIUM
BRITAIN LUX.

Paris

Seine Rhine

G.

Loire Dijon

Nantes SWITZERLAND

FRANCE

Lyon ITALY

Rhône

Bordeaux

Marseille

SPAIN AND.

www.marco-polo.com

SYMBOLS

INSIDERTIP	Insider Tip
★	Highlight
●●●●	Best of...
☆	Scenic view
⊘	Responsible travel: for eco-logical or fair trade aspects
(*)	Telephone numbers that are not toll-free

**PRICE CATEGORIES
HOTELS**

Expensive over 160 euros

Moderate 100–160 euros

Budget under 100 euros

Prices are for two people in a
double room per night without breakfast

**PRICE CATEGORIES
RESTAURANTS**

Expensive over 60 euros

Moderate 35–60 euros

Budget under 35 euros

Prices are for an evening
menu with starter, main
course and dessert, without
wine

CONTENTS

DID YOU KNOW?
Relax & enjoy → p. 38
Keep fit! → p. 43
Books & films → p. 51
Gourmet restaurants → p. 64
Local specialities → p. 70
Into the early hours → p. 86
Luxury hotels → p. 96
Horses – football – tennis → p. 100
National holidays → p. 121
Budgeting → p. 125
Currency converter → p. 127

MAPS IN THE GUIDEBOOK
(136 A1) Page numbers and coordinates refer to the street atlas, the map of the districts and the map of Greater Paris

(0) Site/address located off the map
Coordinates are also given for places that are not marked on the street atlas

(🚇 A1) refers to the removable pull-out map

INSIDE FRONT COVER:
The best Highlights

INSIDE BACK COVER:
Metro-/RER map

The best MARCO POLO Insider Tips

Our top 15 Insider Tips

BEST OF...

GREAT PLACES FOR FREE
Discover new places and save money

● *Atmospheric organ concerts*
A number of churches regularly offer free concerts. The rich sound of organ music resonating through the arches of *Notre-Dame Cathedral* is more than impressive – both visually and acoustically → p. 33

● *Free couscous*
The *Le Tribal-Café* as well as a dozen or so other restaurants provide a free meal on weekends. However, guests are expected to pay a small amount for a beverage. The atmosphere is convivial, as though you were dining with friends → p. 68

● *Free museum admission*
Hard to believe, but true: many museums in Paris do not charge admission. One of the most highly recommended is the *Musée d'Art Moderne de la Ville de Paris* → p. 31

● *Free attractions with a view*
For the best view of the city without paying admission for the Eiffel Tower or the Tour Montparnasse climb the stairs of *Sacré-Cœur*. Performances by jugglers and musicians at no extra cost → p. 57

● *Paris on inline skates*
Every Friday evening, nearly 20 miles of the city are closed off for avid Rollerbladers. Inline skating through Paris is one of the most enjoyable ways of getting to know Paris – if only a small part. The fun begins at 10pm at Montparnasse station (photo) → p. 88

● *Live chansons at no charge*
Even the more modest restaurants frequently provide diners with the opportunity to listen to classic French songs after a good meal – live. Restaurants such as *Le Limonaire* are particularly atmospheric → p. 88

◖◗◖◗ Dots in guidebook refer to "Best of..." tips

● *Gourmet mecca*

Nowhere else in the world have so many stars graced both chefs and restaurants as in Paris. Yet the *brasseries* such as *Bofinger* are still the gastronomic heart of the city, offering the best quality plus an amazing ambiance → **p. 62**

● *Arcades – Nostalgie à la française*

Paris is defined by the splendour of its past. Upscale covered shopping centres such as the *Galerie Vivienne* (photo) have existed since the 18th century and are typical of parts of the city even today → **p. 42**

● *Inner city market with multicultural flair*

Chinese, Indians and Africans from every part of the continent have all injected culture and an exotic flair into certain districts. The African market, *Marché Barbès*, is a tantalising example → **p. 81**

● *Luxurious shopping*

Paris, as the epitome of luxury, is celebrated for its champagne, perfume and fashion. You can find a large selection of luxury items within the "Triangle d'Or" – the golden triangle around the *rue du Faubourg Saint-Honoré* → **p. 78**

● *Museums of international renown*

Alongside the Louvre – the museum with the largest exhibition space in the world – the Centre Pompidou boasts the largest collection of modern art in Europe today. The museum that best reflects Paris, however, is the *Musée d'Orsay,* with its collection of works by the French Impressionists → **p. 39**

● *Street cafés*

Street cafés act as an extension of a Parisian living room. Even the tiniest space on the pavement has enough room for a couple of tables and chairs. The café terrace at the *Café Marly* at the Louvre is ideal for people-watching → **p. 66**

● *Exhibition of the city's history*

There are few cities in Europe that can look back on such a tumultuous 2,000 year history. The *Musée Carnavalet* displays a profound and inspiring insight into the city's past → **p. 47**

ONLY IN

BEST OF...

● *Covered shopping centres*
There are numerous department stores and covered passages that are ideal for souvenir hunting during a downpour. The *Carrousel du Louvre* is architecturally stunning and its shops are open on Sundays → p. 36

● *Jungle in the city*
The *greenhouses* in the Jardin des Plantes are a tribute to the resplendent Belle Époque. The lush vegetation will revive your spirits on a damp rainy day in Paris → p. 119

● *Browse and listen in this bookstore*
You'll need plenty of time to shop for CDs, books and DVDs at the most ideal venue, *Fnac*. It is located on the Champs-Elysées and stays open until midnight → p. 74

● *Museum of foreign cultures*
Have you already ticked off all the "must-sees" from your list of museums? If these didn't include the impressive *Musée Quai Branly,* it's well worth spending an entire day in this foreign cultural environment – and you still won't have seen everything on display → p. 32

● *Be part of the aristocracy in this restaurant*
While away the time until the sun reappears in the midst of gilded pageantry at the most beautiful railway station restaurant in the world, *Le Train Bleu* (photo). You don't even need to have a meal there to experience its grandeur – let yourself be enraptured by the sumptuousness of the comfortable leather chairs → p. 65

● *Go underground*
The "underworld" in Paris is extensive, not only for the Métro and sewage system, but also the *catacombs*, an over 300km (186mi)-long system of tunnels for the dead → p. 54

RAIN

RELAX AND CHILL OUT
Take it easy and spoil yourself

● *Green urban oases*

Paris is known for its parks that are oases of calm in the boisterous city. The most beloved of them is the *Jardin du Luxembourg* (photo), where you can always find a quiet spot to dream → **p. 50**

● *Luxury hotel spa package*

Some luxury hotels offer an all-inclusive pampering package. The *L'Hôtel* is a real gem, complete with hamam and a pool under the arches, reminiscent of an ancient Roman spa → **p. 93**

● *Tranquil beauty in the church courtyard*

Seek contemplation and relaxation among the tombs of famous poets, painters and musicians, surrounded by nature. Paris' cemeteries, especially the lovely *Père Lachaise* with its majestic trees, are the epitome of serenity → **p. 55**

● *Teatime*

Tea is in popular demand. The *Maison de Thé George Cannon* in particular is devoted to this calming and stimulating herb. Once you've tasted the tea on the ground floor, treat yourself to a shiatsu massage. In the basement you'll find not only a tea shop, but also an original Japanese tea ceremony → **p. 76**

● *Relax on the beach*

Every summer the Seine promenades are piled up with sand. When the *Paris plages* open, they are closed to traffic to create a relaxing beach atmosphere in the heart of the city → **p. 120**

● *Picnics along the canal*

A row of bars line the *Canal Saint-Martin* like a strand of pearls, while the banks of the canal have been converted into a huge picnic area. Sitting on the waterfront on a mild summer night offers a particular Parisian flair → **p. 24**

INTRODUCTION

DISCOVER PARIS!

Paris has been called the city of love, fashion, gastronomy, art and even the city of lights. It has always been a metropolis where only the best is good enough, a city of superlatives. Faster, prettier, bigger, glossier than most other cities and definitely on par with major capital cities such as London, New York and Berlin. All it takes is a stroll along the magnificent mile-long Champs-Elysées illuminated by *135 000 lights* on a December evening or a coffee at a street café as you watch the colourful hustle and bustle of the vibrant Saint-Germain-des-Prés district at all hours with its exuberant student life and many nightclubs to be infected by the charm of this city. You can get a good overview of the city from the observation platform on the sixth floor of the Centre Georges Pompidou, which lies in the middle of the city centre and high enough up that you can take in the sea of buildings. The city spreads out like an open history book beneath you. The bright mobile sculptures and cascading water of the Stravinsky Fountain lie at your feet and, further up, the towers of the famous Notre-Dame Cathedral loom into view. It stands on the Île de la Cité, the

Strolling along the Champs-Elysées at the foot of the Arc de Triomphe

actual nucleus of the city where the Parisii settled in the 3rd century BC. A bit further afield you'll recognise the defiant towers of the former prison, la Conciergerie. Even further beyond and slightly to the right, you can see the sprawling giant complex of the Louvre, a former royal palace that now houses the *largest museum in the world*. To the right behind you is the sparkling golden dome of Les Invalides in which Napoleon found his final resting place. Not far away the symbol of the city, the Eiffel Tower, looms on the horizon. To the far right and to the west you can pick out the high-rises in La Défense, *Europe's largest office district*. Look further to the right and north to where the dazzling white church, Sacré-Cœur, crowns the highest peak of the former artists' hill, Montmartre.

Paris has been the vibrant political, economical and cultural epicentre of France for centuries and one of the largest metropolises in the world. As the residence of kings and the seat of government and by virtue of its numerous universities, Paris was also recognised as an *intellectual centre in Europe* as far back as the Middle Ages. It has been the workplace for countless artists, writers and architects and a continual source of unrest and uprisings. Paris was the stage for many revo-

> **Paris has been the stage for many revolutions**

lutions. The great revolution of 1789, known for its motto "liberty, equality, fraternity", even became a symbol for the fight against oppression, although the rights championed mostly benefited the bourgeoisie and not the lower classes. Nevertheless, the French Revolution became a guiding light for freedom movements in many countries.

Strikes and demonstrations still frequently occur in Paris and, even if they no longer have universal historical significance, every French government still fears mobilisation in the streets. The challenges associated with a large, congested urban area – metropolitan Paris has a population of 11 million – are comparable with those of other cities of the same size. Huge traffic and environmental issues, lavish restoration projects and prohibitive rents, which continuously banish the socially vulnerable and the immigrants to the dreary apartment blocks in the suburbs, are ongoing struggles in Paris.

And yet the city has survived so much upheaval and so many political revolutions and crises without losing any of its fascination. What gives Paris its special flair? For some, it's the *grand boulevards* so ideal for strolling. For others it's the lure of luxury boutiques on the rue du Faubourg Saint-Honoré or shopping in *world-enowned department stores* such as Galeries Lafayette or Printemps, famed for their extravagant Christmas decorations. Others are content to explore the incredible variety of *museums of international renown*, sit in a street café or relax in one of the many parks – or just go with the flow.

Even the older, the provincial, almost rural and unvarnished Paris still exists: attractive alleyways, crooked little buildings with cafés or pleasant restaurants, shops with enticing displays and chattering shopkeepers, the hubbub of activity wherever fresh produce is delivered, and *fascinating markets* with their typically colourful displays of fruit and vegetables, cheese, sausages and meat, pastries and cakes whose vendors loudly tout their wares. This folksy side of Paris

Famous department stores and museums of international renown

is typical north and east of the city, for example in Belleville, which, similar to the Goutte d'Or district, is inhabited by a large number of immigrants. Even the hills of Butte-aux-Cailles have partially retained their old Paris charm with bistros and restaurants that attract a young crowd.

Paris has always had a colourful mixture of people from various backgrounds. Centuries ago, it was the Bretons, Auvergneses, Alsatians and Basques who came to Paris in search of a better life that enriched the city – it was the Alsatians who first introduced their brasseries. Much later, Africans arrived who maintain a wonderfully colourful market in Goutte d'Or every Sunday, and the Chinese, who settled in Place d'Italie where they opened their businesses and restaurants.

Paris is multicultural and tolerant. The city opened its arms to the politically persecuted, as well as revolutionaries such as Karl Marx and Leo Trotsky, and granted asylum to refugees from Nazi Germany. It is a city that has always attracted artists and it is no coincidence that *major art movements* such as Impressionism and Cubism found their beginnings here. Painters like Auguste Renoir, Vincent van Gogh and Pablo Picasso as well as writers such as Voltaire, Victor Hugo, Honoré de Balzac, Charles Baudelaire, Marcel Proust, Ernest Hemingway and Jean-Paul Sartre lived and worked here. Artists met in cafés and brasseries that have since become famous on the

Paris is multicultural and tolerant

left of the Seine – the *rive gauche.* This area, around the university buildings of the Sorbonne, has long been the *intellectual heart* of the city. The majority of these meeting places such as Procope, Le Flore, or the existentialists' rendezvous Les Deux Magots in the Quartier Latin, and the Closerie des Lilas in the former artists' district of Montparnasse, still exist today. These cafés and restaurants are a welcome place to stop by, especially for tourists and the well-heeled. But they, like the rest of the affluent metropolis, have long since become too expensive for poor poets and struggling artists.

Paris, with its capricious beauty, was home to all sectors of society for centuries, but it is now increasingly becoming a *museum city*, a capital for the rich and beautiful, rendered virtually unaffordable for the average citizen who has to make do with a tiny flat. A cappuccino can easily cost more than 5 euros, an evening meal served with wine, 60 euros or more. The extravagantly ornate palace façades with their grand entrances and marble staircases characteristic of the Haussmann era often conceal shabby backstairs and cramped attic rooms lacking in proper insulation, which are ice cold in winter and boiling hot in summer. These *chambres des bonnes*, the former servants' quarters, are now rented out to students or even teachers transferred to Paris from the provinces – $13m^2$ for up to 1,000 euros per month – and often without a WC and shower, albeit with a view of Sacré-Cœur or the Eiffel Tower. The government is now demanding a tax penalty for rents over 40 euros/m^2. However, in light of the shortage of *social housing*, this situation is likely to continue. And so the Parisians' daily struggle against high prices, congested streets, crowded public transportation, crime and filth goes on – although most of them are proud of their city.

Many old buildings in Paris have been and continue to be torn down, which always means the irrevocable loss of the city's architectural history. New, ambitious projects are aimed ostensibly at making the city centre a place to live in again. Traffic is being curtailed by *transport restriction schemes*, new green and recreation areas along the Seine are being created, public transportation modernised and artists' colonies established. La Défense, the business district situated to the west of the city gates with its skyscrapers is slated for expansion, high-rises are planned along the edge of the inner ring road and Parisians themselves are hotly debating whether skyscrapers should be built right in the middle of the city to give Paris the look of a real, modern metropolis.

All of this urban development will once again alter the face of a city that has already seen so many changes. The former President François Mitterrand, who launched

The Jardins du Trocadéro with the bull and fawn sculpture by Paul Jouve near the the Eiffel Tower

his "Grands Projets" including the glass pyramid at the Louvre, the Grande Arche at La Défense, the Opéra Bastille and the Très Grande Bibliothèque (completed under his successor Jacques Chirac), once said: "You cannot have great politics without great architecture". However, architecture and large projects today have to meet the needs of the citizens. The focus is on making Paris a better place to live in, as opposed to erecting new buildings for reasons of prestige. Many young residents prefer to spend weekends in London, Barcelona, Amsterdam or Berlin where life seems more glamorous than in Paris. Yet in the past the city has always proven that it is capable of reinventing itself. Such resilience will carry Parisians confidently into the future.

No great politics without great architecture

WHAT'S HOT

1 Freshly roasted

Coffee France is rediscovering coffee thanks to the growing popularity of coffee shops that roast their own beans among young Parisians. Courses and tastings akin to wine seminars are even offiered at *Caféotheque (52, rue de l'Hôtel de Ville | www.lacafeotheque.com)*. The coffee is also freshly roasted at *Café Lomi (3, rue Marcadet | cafelomi.com)*. Snacks such as banana bread and select cheeses are the perfect accompaniment to the *grand crus.* The stylish café *Coutume (47, rue de Babylone)* also stocks a huge selection of coffees.

2 Art to go

Spontaneous creativity Spontaneity can be ulltra hip. Websites such as *www.la-boutique-ephemere. com* announce last-minute art and design sales at spontaneously determined places within Paris. *Art éphémèmere,* i.e. street art or murals on buildings, is particularly popular. The often witty stencil art *(pochoirs)* on the streets of Paris is always worth a second look. An overview of these popular art genres can be found at *www.trompe-l-oeil.info* or *urbanart-paris.fr*.

3 Your very own scent

Perfume An increasing number of French women are emphasizing their individuality by creating their own perfumes. In special ateliers *(www.abcduparfum.fr)* or *(www.cinquiemesens.com)*, you can learn the secrets that go into making a fine Eau de Toilette. After a three hour course in perfume and scents course, you'll go home with your very own signature scent. At *Lilou Store (145, Blvd. Saint-Germain | lilouparis.com)* you can also accessorize your outfit with self-designed jewellery.

More than a meal

Experimental dining Given that culinary artistry has been perfected to the extreme in Paris over the centuries, the focus has now been shifted to the dining experience itself. First came a meal in the dark *(www.danslenoir.com)* and a huge picnic with everyone clad in white *(dinerenblanc.info)*, then came eating to the sounds of an Italian opera *(www.lebelcanto.com)*. Now it is all the rage to eat in complete silence. Three hundred people signed up for the first silent meal – within chic surroundings, of course, and at a price of 100 euros per person per evening *(www.ledinerensilence.com)*. Let's wait and see how long this trend will last because the French notoriously love to talk about their food!

Concept stores

Shopping Trendsetters will find just what they are looking for in so-called "concept stores" in which fashion, shoes, home accessories, books, cosmetics and music are all rolled into one. These shops, such as *SoWe-Are (40, rue de Charonne | soweare-shop.fr)* or the large but seemingly modest *Centre Commercial (2, rue de Marseille | www.centrecommercial.cc)* are popping up all over the place with shelves stocked with unusual labels from France, England and Denmark. Classic French designers such as Christian Lacroix have followed suit with *boutique nouvelle generation* such as *Mix and Match (24, Place Sulpice)* in a former printing house.

IN A NUTSHELL

CHAMPS-ELYSÉES

A lot of major companies clamour for a place on what is often referred to as the most beautiful avenue in the world. The upper section, around the Arc de Triomphe, belongs to luxury brand names such as Guerlain, Cartier and Hugo Boss. The star among the flagship stores as well as the top tourist attraction is the home of the leather goods manufacturer, Louis Vuitton. A specially designed "walk" through the shop leads you past spectacular light and video installations and contemporary works of art. Ever since Abercrombie & Fitch set up shop here, its Art Deco palace behind golden doors has become a magnet for young fashion fans. Not far away, Nespresso has opened a 5,600 ft² location with a bar for a quick espresso, a lounge and a VIP area. Further down, just before you reach the haute couture street Avenue Montaigne, you can't help but notice the Adidas flagship store with its black and white exterior. Its competitor Nike has had a store here for years. Citroën has opened an avante-garde showroom made of glass and steel a few yards away. Even Renault, Toyota and Daimler use this prestigious location to their advantage to display prototypes, Formula 1 racing cars, spectacular installations – and also for entertaining guests.

LES HALLES

The construction site at the former market halls in the heart of Paris plagued the city for over six years. None-

Attractions that make Paris a city worth experiencing – day in, day out

theless, the major transportation hub of Châtelet-Les Halles through which almost a million passagengers stream daily was hardly effected by this undertaking. At the end of the 1970s, the produce trade in the city was relocated from these legendary market halls to Rungis, making way for a shopping centre within the old buildings. Just thirty years later, the safety of the halls could no longer be guaranteed. Now, thanks to the extensive renovations, the crowds of visitors passing through can expect a better infrastructure. The canopy made of glass elegantly connects the underbelly with the quartier above. A number of public cultural institutions and new landscaped gardens are planned as part of the efforts to revive the entire neighbourhood.

LES PUCES

Paris' flea markets, especially the *Marché aux Puces de Saint-Ouen* at the Porte de Clignancourt, are a major attraction in the metropolis. Every year, more than five million people visit the largest antique market in the world which actually consists of 16 individual markets, open only from Saturday to Monday. In, and in front of, the many multi-level halls you can choose between clothing, various odds-and-ends and even a huge range of furniture. Every hall has its own theme – from Art Nouveau to the Seventies. At the end of the 19th century the market was driven out of Paris, but flourished on the northern edge of the city for many decades. Many foreigners – predominantly American – are among the market's most important customers.

For a number of years now, business has been floundering. Many of its vendors are no longer making high enough sales and an ever increasing number have given up entirely. The downturn began following the absence of Americans as a result of the September 11 attacks, and continued to slow down during the financial crisis.

What is more, high-end vendors have turned to the more costly antique shops in Saint-Germain-des-Prés or from the auction house Drouot, while the lower-end segment has sufferef from competition from private flea markets and the Internet.

For tourists, however, it's still a treat to wander around the various stands outside or through the halls, with the hope of finding a few bargains. And an unuusual souvenir is always a nice reminder of a holiday in Paris. Despite discussions about the future of flea markets there have also been some interesting new developments. In some of the halls, restaurants have become established, some even with jazz music.

MACARONS

They are more than just cookies as they seem to embody the French way of life. These small, round, pastel or brightly-coloured meringue tidbits made with almond flour are served af-

Macarons are more than just a trend – they are simply delightful!

ter dinner or at teatime by anyone who is anyone in France. Of course, they must come from *Ladurée* (see p. 63) or *Pierre Hermé* (www.pierreherme.com), the best addresses in the city for these fine creations (approx. 2 euros each). A macaron was a rather dry affair until the mid-20th century when the idea of splitting them in half to spread a creamy filling in between was born.

Nowadays, the queues outside the bright-green boutiques of Ladurée which resemble 18th-century tea shops are almost always long. It is estimated that Ladurée's annual sales jumpred from 3 million euros in 1993 to 140 million euros in 2012. Alongside classic variations such as chocolate, vanilla, coffee, orange blossom and rosewater, most shops offer seasonal flavours such as cinnamon or violet. The queen of lingerie Chantal Thomass designed the little aprons worn by the Ladurée shopgirls, but the boxes in which the macarons are packed within silk paper are redone by a different fashion designer every year.

Entrance of the métro station Saint-Michel

MÉTRO STATIONS

Although it is not the oldest underground railway system in the world (it first opened in 1900), it is certainly one of the most densely knit networks. There is supposedly nowhere in Paris further than 1,900 feet from one of the 300 stations. After all, Paris would not be Paris without he famous wrought iron Art Nouveau Métro entrances by the artist Hector Guimard (1867–1942).

The arabesque-shaped *bouche du metro* (mouth of the Métro) at the station *Porte Dauphine* is particularly eye-catching with its flowers in the form of red lamps that grow out of the vine-like ironwork. The modern counterpart to the some 80 Guimard entrances is the glass masterpiece *kiosque des noctambules*, the night owls' pavilion, created by Jean-Michel Othoniel. It graces the entrance to the station *Palais Royal-Musée de Louvre* on the square in front of the Comedie Française with its colourful spheres of murano glass. Tastefully illuminated statues point the way to the largest museum in the world underground at the Louvre station. A replica of *The Thinker* sits in the station *Varenne*, marking its proximity to the Musée Rodin. The *Arts et Metier* station, clad entirely in copper with huge cogwheels echoing the days of steam engines, is considered one of the most beautiful in the city. A wall mural at the *Bastille* station commemorates the mercurial history of the site. The *Cluny-Sorbonne* station has been embellished with beautiful mosaics by Jean René Bazaine, and its ceiling bears the names of famous former students of the nearby university.

MODERN ART

There is hardly a city in the world that can boast as many museums as Paris. Contemporary art used to live a peripheral existence and artists had to eke out a living in an exorbitantly expensive city. This has changed since the inauguration of the international contemporary art fair FIAC which takes place every year in October, as well as exhibitions at the *Palais de Tokyo* where modern art has be given a forum. *Centquatre (www.104.fr)*, a gigantic hall covered with a 19th-century glass roof, provides flats and studios for artists as well as shops, a restaurant, café and concert halls. The establishment of the *Fondation Louis Vuitton* (see p. 55) as a forum for contemporary art in Bois de Boulogne by the luxury corporation LVMH in 2014 has further boosted efforts in this regard.

NIGHTLIFE

The Moulin Rouge, cabarets, jazz clubs, the Pigalle red-light district and discos such as Les Bains Douches: Paris nightlife is legendary. But its glory has faded. Many tourists as well as locals have been ripped off. Even if you pass the strict dress code, you will need a great deal of cash: the cover charge can be as high as 30 euros, and expect to shell out a minimum of another 10 euros for a drink voucher. Increasingly strict regulations as a result of residents' complaints, the early closure of the Métro, the lack of taxis and expensive parking fees mean that most everyone goes home by 2am.

PICNIC

Parisians enjoy sitting outdoors. But in the light of increasingly high costs many residents and tourists have discovered the simple pleasure of a picnic at the appearance of the first rays of sunshine. A favourite sport is the pedestrian bridge, *Pont des Arts*, which has a view towards the Louvre and Île de la Cité and, on warm evenings, there is rarely any enough space. The same holds true for the parks around the Eiffel Tower.

The sunlit quays on the Seine are even more popular, especially in the afternoon. On Sunday there are also sections closed to traffic which are otherwise quite busy. A unique vista is the shadowy western tip of the island, *Île de la Cité*, especially at dusk, although it is usually crowded at this time. The romantically inclined and dance freaks often picnic on the Seine quay, *Saint-Bernard*, (left of the Seine, between Île de la Cité and Austerlitz station). Salsa and tango dancing are popular in the early evening around the small inlets directly on the river (free).

In the afternoon and late into the evening, picnicking can also be recommended along the ● INSIDER TIP *Canal*

Temporary exhibitions in the Palais de Tokyo are dedicated to modern art

Saint-Martin. Signs along the romantic, tree-lined waterways ask people not to picnic after 9pm, so as not to disturb the residents, but few heed the message. It is common for picnickers to spread out their blankets late in the evening as they eat baguettes, cheese, pasties and quiches washed down with cider, wine or beer. A picnic is an economical and romantic affair in a typically Parisian atmosphere.

WITHOUT A CAR

Paris is choked to death by the traffic. The Boulevard Périphérique is not the only ring road notorious for traffic jams. Even the roads built along the Seine in the 1960s and 1970s are susceptible to gridlocks. Whenever the hot air balloon over the Parc Citroën changes its colour to red, the air in the metropolis has become so dirty that it can be a danger to health. It is therefore no surprise that the mayor, Anne Hidalgo, wants to ban car traffic from the city centre as much as possible. Step-by-step, the four central districts are supposed to become strictly controlled traffic areas, and vehicles with diesel motors are to be banned completely by 2020. A viable alternative to a car is the bike rental system *Velib* (see p. 125) with its over 20,000 grey bikes at over 1,800 stations around the city. For longer distances, many Parisians favour the small electric cars of the *Autolib* system that can be rented along the same lines as the bicycles. In and around Paris, it has 3,000 cars that can be rented at 1,000 different stations.

Without a doubt, the closure of the streets along the Seine to motor vehicle traffic has contributed greatly to better air quality and health in the city centre. Building on the success of the annual *Paris Plages* event (see p. 120) and the partial blockade of the right bank, a 2.3 km (1.4 mile) stretch along the left bank between the *Musée du Quai Branly* and the *Musée d'Orsay* has been turned into *Les Berges* (www.lesberges.fr) with floating gardens, bars, restaurants, kids' activities, lounge chairs, floating stages for films and concerts, and free fitness courses all year round.

SIGHTSEEING

Whether you're set on visiting the major attractions, on the lookout for the most spectacular squares and expensive shops, or seeking the charm of "old Paris" with its winding lanes, what you make of your stay in Paris is entirely up to you.

Paris is divided into 20 arrondissements. In order to provide a better overview, they have been categorised into five areas in this guidebook. Find the one that best suits you – and bear in mind that a combination of museum visits and outdoor activities is often the best balance.

One thing is for sure: you'll never be bored in Paris. To prevent your exploration of the city from becoming too much, it's well worth seeking out one of the magnificent parks or relaxing in one of the numerous cafés to get a real

WHERE TO START?
Paris is large, and there is no so-called city centre. For a proper overview, it's best to take the Métro line M 2 to **Anvers (141 D5)** (*L4*). As soon as the train is above ground, you'll see Sacré-Cœur. Once you've scaled the steps, you'll have Paris at your feet. For a close-up of the Île de la Cité and the Louvre the (admittedly complex) Métro/RER railway station **Châtelet-Les Halles (147 D–E5)** (*M8*) is the ideal starting point.

Superlative sites and smaller treasures to discover: Paris has much more to offer than the Eiffel Tower, the Louvre and Notre-Dame

feel for the Parisian way of life. People-watching is often an activity in itself. If you're tired of walking, the bus route 73 will take you past La Défense and the Arc de Triomphe, down the Champs-Elysées and around the Place de la Concorde up to the Musée d'Orsay, and passes an array of sights on the way: an economical and comfortable means of taking in the city.

Paris is a city of museums, with some 160 in total. In the larger ones it's best just to pick out a few sections to visit.

Anyone who capitulates in the face of the sometimes very extensive collections – in the Louvre, you would have to walk some 17km (10½mi) to see everything – can visit one of the many smaller city palaces which are often veritable treasure troves. Note that most of the city's museums are closed on Mondays, while many national museums are closed on Tuesdays.

The "Paris Museum Pass" allows you to visit 60 museums and other places of interest (two days: 42 euros, four

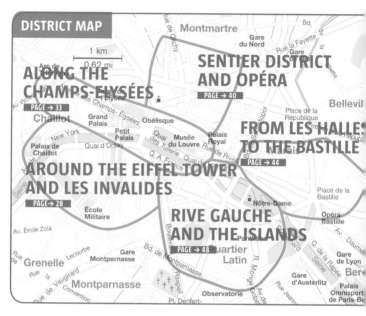

DISTRICT MAP

1 km
0.62 mi

Montmartre
Gare du Nord
Gare

ALONG THE CHAMPS-ÉLYSÉES
PAGE → 33

Chaillot
Grand Palais
Petit Palais
Obélisque
New York
Quai d'Orsay
Palais de Chaillot
Quai Musée des Tuileries du Louvre
Palais Royal
Rue de Rivoli

SENTIER DISTRICT AND OPÉRA
PAGE → 40

Place de la République
Bellevil

FROM LES HALLES TO THE BASTILLE
PAGE → 44

AROUND THE EIFFEL TOWER AND LES INVALIDES
PAGE→ 28

École Militaire

Av. Émile Zola

RIVE GAUCHE AND THE ISLANDS
PAGE → 48
uartier Latin

Notre-Dame
Place de la Bastille
Opéra Bastille

Grenelle
Lecourbe
Gare Montparnasse
Bd. de Montparnasse
Rue de Vaugirard
Convention
Montparnasse
Raspail
Observatoire
Pl. Denfert-

Gare de Lyon
Gare d'Austerlitz
Palais Omnisport de Paris-B
Ber

The map shows the location of the most interesting districts. There is a detailed map of each district on which each of the sights described is numbered.

days: 56 euros, six days: 69 euros). You can obtain the pass at the Office du Tourisme (see p. 126), in Fnac stores, at major Métro stations and online. Incidentally, many museums are free on the first Sunday of the month. Most places offer discounts for students and senior citizens – EU passport holders under 26, for example, have free admission to all national museums *(musées nationaux)* in the city. *www.parismuseumpass.com, www. fnac.com, www.rmn.fr*

AROUND THE EIFFEL TOWER AND LES INVALIDES

Paris Ouest has long been the area preferred by the wealthier classes. The 16th arrondissement on the other side of the Seine and the 7th arrondissement between the Eiffel Tower and Les Invalides are among the most exclusive addresses in the city.

The elegant streets with consulates, ministries and several beautiful palaces are relatively calm and the pace more leisurely. Tourists crowd around this area to see the Eiffel Tower, the city's major landmark. INSIDER TIP The most popular photo opportunity, however, is on the other side of the Seine, from the vestibule of the Palais de Chaillot, whose side wings accommodate a museum and a theatre *(www.theatre-chaillot.fr)*. The most popular museum there is the *Cité de l'Architecture et du Patrimoine (www. citechaillot.fr)*, in which the work of prominent French architects and their buildings from the 12th century onwards are exhibited.

You can INSIDER TIP avoid the lengthy queue in front of the Eiffel tower by booking a 3½-hour city tour with *Paris City Vision (www.pariscityvision.com)*. The tour costs 59 euros and includes admission to the Eiffel Tower and a fast-track queue. Or make a reservation (weeks in advance!) at one of the restaurants in the tower and enjoy the privilege of a private lift. You have a choice between *Jules Verne* (see p. 64) or the less pricey *58 Tour Eiffel (daily | tel. 0145 55 20 04 | www.restaurants-toureiffel.com | Moderate–Expensive)* on the first floor. And if you don't want to wait or dine, take a look at the tower from below and stroll through the nearby park to the end of the Esplanade des Invalides where Napoleon's tomb resides in Les Invalides.

■1 EIFFEL TOWER (TOUR EIFFEL) ★
☆ (144 B5) (*Ω F8*)

Paris would not be Paris without the Eiffel Tower. The 300 m high (985 ft) landmark long held the distinction as the highest structure in the world. Built by Gustave Eiffel on the occasion of the 100-year anniversary of the French Revolution and the World Exposition in

1889, the steel structure was initially highly controversial. The tower was originally only meant to stay there for 20 years. But, because of its importance as a weather station and later for air traffic as well as a radio and television station, it was allowed to remain.

The second platform, at a height of 115 m (380 ft), provides an impressive panoramic view over Paris; from the highest level at 274 m (900 ft), the view on a clear day extends right across the whole Paris basin. If you would like, you can INSIDER**TIP** ▶ sip a glass of champagne on the platform (from 12 euros). *Daily 9am–midnight, 17 June–29 Aug 9am–12.45am, stairs until 6pm or midnight | lift/stairs to 2nd floor 9/7.50 euros, 3rd floor 15.50/13.50 euros | 5, av. Gustave Eiffel | 7th arr. | M Tour Eiffel | RER C | www.tour-eiffel.fr*

2 INVALIDES (145 E5–6) (*ω G–H8*)

The *Hôtel des Invalides* is, after the palace at Versailles, the largest building complex constructed during the reign of Louis XIV. The "Sun King" had it erected for his wounded war veterans. In order to prevent the ex-soldiers from becoming beggars or thieves, he set up special workshops governed by strict discipline to provide up to 3,000 invalids with work and good care. In addition to the soldiers' church, the Baroque *Dôme des Invalides* with its shining golden cupola is the main attraction. *Napoleon's tomb* reigns over the area beneath the dome. The annexed *Army Museum*, founded in 1794, is one of the largest of its kind in the world and testifies to the glory of the French Army. *Daily, April–Sept 10am–6pm, Oct–March 10am–5pm (Tue until 9pm) | admission 9.50 euros | Esplanade*

Les Invalides is the site of Napoleon's tomb which consists of six interlocking coffins

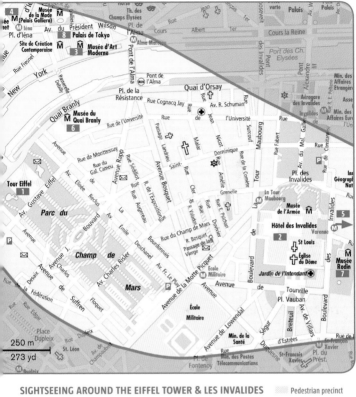

SIGHTSEEING AROUND THE EIFFEL TOWER & LES INVALIDES ▨ Pedestrian precinct

1 Tour Eiffel

2 Invalides

3 Musée d'Art Moderne de la Ville de Paris

4 Musée Guimet (Musée National des Arts Asiatiques)

5 Musée Maillol

6 Musée du Quai Branly

7 Musée Rodin

8 Palais de Tokyo

des Invalides | 7th arr. | M 8 La Tour-Maubourg | M 13 Varenne | www.invalides.org

3 MUSÉE D'ART MODERNE DE LA VILLE DE PARIS ● (144 C4) (ᗱ F7)

The museum reopened several years ago after extensive renovations. Among the exhibits of modern art (Fernand Léger, Robert Delaunay, Pablo Picasso, Georges Braque and Amedeo Modigliani), you can admire Raoul Dufy's *Fée Electricité* (the largest painting in the world) and *La Danse* by Henri Matisse. Stunning view from the ☆ terrace of the museum restaurant – the salads are highly recommended – over the Seine to the Eiffel Tower nearby. *Tue–Sun 10am–6pm (Thu until 10pm) | free admission (temporary exhibitions 5–12 euros) | 11, av. du Président*

Part of the bronze sculpture "The Gates of Hell" in the garden at the Musée Rodin

*Wilson | 16th arr. | M 9 Iéna | www.mam.
paris.fr*

◢ MUSÉE GUIMET (MUSÉE NATIONAL DES ARTS ASIATIQUES)
(144 B3) (*ℳ F6–7*)

With its extraordinarily extensive collection of Asian art, the museum provides an intensively vivid picture of the Far East and its religions. Selected objects from India, China, Japan, Indonesia and Tibet are displayed here. *Wed–Mon 10am–6pm | admission 7.50 euros | 6, place d'Iéna | 16th arr. | M 9 Iéna | www. guimet.fr*

◢ MUSÉE MAILLOL (146 A6) (*ℳ J8*)

Dina Vierny, the founder of the museum and a former model, assembled this testimony to the ground-breaking sculptor and painter Aristide Maillol (1861–1944) and his elegant works. 18 female sculptures by Maillol are also featured in the *Jardin des Tuileries*. *Wed–Mon 10:30am–7pm | admission 11 euros | 59–61, rue de Grenelle | 7th arr. | M 12 rue du Bac | www. museemaillol.com*

◢ MUSÉE DU QUAI BRANLY ●
(144 C4) (*ℳ F7*)

The museum designed by the renowned architect Jean Nouvel at the base of the Eiffel Tower provides an extensive overview of non-European culture. The exhibitions are attractively displayed with more than a hundred video and multimedia installations to stimulate any inquisitive visitor. Special events are also regularly held, e.g. theatre, dance and music. *Tue, Wed, Sun 11am–7pm, Thu, Fri, Sat 11am–9pm | admission 10 euros | 37, Quai Branly | 7th arr. | M 9 Iéna | RER C Pont de l'Alma | www. quaibranly.fr*

◢ MUSÉE RODIN (145 E–F6) (*ℳ H8*)

No less a luminary than the German poet Rainer Maria Rilke, who temporarily worked as Auguste Rodin's private secretary, persuaded him to settle in this grand city palace. In addition to famous works such as *The Kiss* or *The Cathedral*, some works by his gifted pupil and lover, Camille Claudel, can also be seen here. The adjoining sculpture park and café are a perfect place to relax, surrounded by art. *Tue–Sun 10am– 5:45pm (Wed until 8:45pm), park until 5pm (in summer until 6:45pm) | admission 10.80 euros (park 1 euro) | 77, rue de Varenne | 7th arr. | M 13 Varenne | www. musee-rodin.fr*

■8■ **PALAIS DE TOKYO** (144 C3) *(ฤ F7)*
Not a museum in the classical sense. Contemporary artists present their sometimes provocative and giant installations in temporary exhibitions within the halls constructed for the 1937 World Exposition near the Eiffel Tower. The café *Tokyo Idem,* reminiscent of a modest canteen, is considered ultra-trendy by young Parisians. *Wed–Mon noon–midnight | admission 10 euros | 13, av. du Président Wilson | 16th arr. | M 9 Iéna | www.palaisdetokyo.com*

ALONG THE CHAMPS-ELYSÉES

The famed and prestigious Champs-Elysées is a part of a vista which begins at the small arch of the Carrousel du Louvre, continues to the middle arch of the Arc de Triomphe and then ends to the west at the giant, modern, Grande Arche de La Défense.
Traffic on the multiple-lane grand boulevard is hectic day and night. Pandemonium also rules among the masses of

tourists who spill out onto the broad pavements every season. In the boutiques, some of which are open until midnight, and in the numerous cafés, the motto "see and be seen" prevails. In order to uphold this standard, the city authorities have adopted a policy limiting the number of cheap chain stores that are permitted to settle in this coveted area. The grand boulevard is intersected at the lower end by the Avenue Montaigne, one of the most expensive addresses when it comes to fashion. The glass palaces, the Grand and Petit Palais, erected in 1900 on the occasion of the

LOW BUDGET

Every Saturday from 8pm to 9pm, a free organ concert is held in ● Notre-Dame **(147 E6)** *(ฤ M9)*. *www.cathe draledeparis.com*

Under *www.paris.fr/musees* you'll find information on museums offering free admission all year round, including the Musée Carnavalet, the Maison de Victor Hugo, the perfume museum Fragonard, the Musée de la Vie Romantique and the Musée d'Art Moderne.

Lovers of modern architecture are advised to take a special bus trip to *La Défense* (see p. 56) and the free museum dedicated to its construction history: under *www.ratp.fr,* you can select an *Archi-Bus* line and download brochures for each of the 15 structures described for all twelve suggested bus lines. The informative bus tour costs the same as normal bus fare: 1.70 euros.

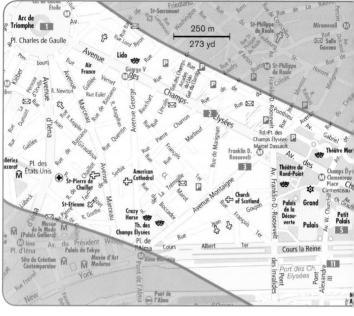

SIGHTSEEING ALONG THE CHAMPS-ÉLYSÉES

1 Arc de Triomphe
2 Avenue des Champs-Elysées
3 Avenue Montaigne
4 Carrousel du Louvre
5 Grand & Petit Palais
6 Jardin des Tuileries
7 Musée du Louvre
8 Musée de l'Orangerie
9 Musée d'Orsay
10 Place de la Concorde
11 Pont Alexandre III

Pedestrian precinct

World Exposition, are located in this section lined by luxuriant greenery, along with the Palais de la Découverte which now houses a science museum.

Don't forget to make a detour to the right of the Louvre in the direction of Pont Alexandre III. From this vantage point you can really appreciate the splendour so typical of the Napoleonic era and the Belle Époque, and it is not difficult to imagine why people flocked to the World Exposition from far and wide to admire the splendour of this city. If you're game for another round of sightseeing, cross the Place de la Con-corde and stroll down the elegant rue Royale to the church of Sainte-Maria Madeleine (La Madeleine). If you would rather relax instead, catch your breath in the Jardin des Tuileries then make your way to the adjacent Louvre.

1 ARC DE TRIOMPHE ★
(144 B–C1) (*F5*)

The 50 m high (165 ft) landmark created by Jean François Chalgrin, based on buildings from Antiquity, rises up along the impressive axis drawn between the small arch of the Louvre and the large arch of La Défense. After Napoleon commissioned the building in 1806 in honour of his "great army" and his victory at the Battle of Austerlitz, it took another 30 years until it was finished. Under the arch, which features important reliefs, including "La Marseillaise", you will find the *Tombe du Soldat Inconnu* (tomb of the unknown soldier), the starting point for the military parade held every year on 14 July.

An underground passage near the Métro station at the Place Charles de Gaulle-

■2 AVENUE DES CHAMPS-ELYSÉES
(144 C–F 2–3) (*ⵓ F–H 5–6*)

The allegedly most beautiful street in the world is not particularly appreciated by Parisians since it is teeming with tourists between the Arc de Triomphe and Place de la Concorde. There are lengthy queues of tourists and locals alike in the evenings and especially at weekends in front of the large cinemas featuring premieres. While the upper

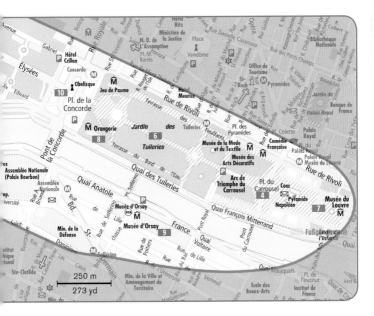

Étoile leads past a small museum on the history of the Arc de Triomphe and the entrance to the ※ viewing platform. You should by no means miss this phenomenal view: no less than a dozen avenues radiate out from the monument in the shape of a star. *Daily, April–Sept 10am–11pm, Oct–March 10am–10:30pm | 9.50 euros | M 1, 2, 6 | RER A Charles de Gaulle-Etoile | www.arc-de-triomphe.monuments-nationaux.fr*

part of the avenue consists of fast food chains and other businesses, the magnificence of the Belle Époque is evident further down.

A short detour to the *Avenue de Marigny* leads you directly to the front of the Elysée Palace, the president's residence. Famous addresses on the mile-long grand boulevard are the elegant perfumery *Guérlain* (no. 68), the renowned dance theatre *Lido* (no. 116), the CD and bookstore *Virgin*

Megastore (nos. 52–60) as well as the exclusive boutique, *Louis Vuitton (no. 101). 8th arr. | M 1 George V | M 1, 9 Franklin D. Roosevelt | M 1, 13 Champs-Elysées-Clemenceau*

▣ AVENUE MONTAIGNE
(145 D3) (*ฌ G6*)

The city's stretch of luxury boutiques, a side street of the Champs-Elysées, is where you'll find nearly every notable fashion designer (Versace, Ricci, Dior and Lacroix), jewellers, perfumeries and leather goods stores. It is not uncommon for customers to be brought to the entrance by their chauffeurs where they are then greeted by white-gloved porters. If you can afford to stay in a luxury hotel, try the *Plaza Athénée*. You will also find the *Théâtre des Champs-Elysées (no. 15)* with its beautiful façade designed by Antoine Bourdelle on this street. *8th arr. | M 1, 9 Franklin D. Roosevelt*

▣ CARROUSEL DU LOUVRE ●
(146 C4) (*ฌ K8*)

The shopping arcade has existed since 1990. The passages under the glass pyramid and the Louvre provide a venue for upscale shops as well as restaurants and cafés. This is the ideal place to take cover during a walk on a rainy Sunday or **INSIDER TIP** to purchase last-minute gifts for friends and family back home. The *Boutique des Musées Nationaux* offers reproductions of works of art from various French museums plus a choice selection of cards and books. An eatery that offers a different style of refreshment after a long stroll: *Restorama (Budget)* serves specialities from all over the world. *Daily 10am–8pm | 1st arr. | M 1, 7 Palais Royal-Musée du Louvre | www.carrouseldulouvre.com*

▣ GRAND & PETIT PALAIS
(145 E3) (*ฌ H6*)

Both palaces were constructed for the 1900 World Exposition and their opulent and historicised decorative sculptures symbolise one of the most flourishing cultural epochs of Paris. The iron and glass construction and domes are jewels of Art Nouveau and Belle Époque style. While the *Grand Palais (changing opening hours | av. Winston-Churchill | www.grandpalais.fr)* exclusively hosts first rate temporary exhibitions, the lavishly restored *Petit Palais (Tue–Sun 10am–6pm, Thu until 8pm | 3, av. du Général Eisenhower | www.petitpalais. paris.fr)* has a permanent exhibition with artworks and paintings from the 18th and 19th centuries (free admission). *8th arr. | M 1, 13 Champs-Elysées-Clemenceau*

▣ JARDIN DES TUILERIES
(146 A–B 3–4) (*ฌ J–K7*)

Regarded as the "front garden" of the Louvre, this Baroque park has existed

since 1666. It was one of the first parks opened to the general public and became a model for many other parks in Europe. Especially noteworthy are the 18 statues of women by Aristide Maillol, which seem almost surreal peeking out between the carefully manicured hedges. *1st arr. | M 1, 8, 12 Concorde | M 1 Tuileries*

7 MUSÉE DU LOUVRE ⭐
(146 C4–5) (*∅ K–L7*)

A well thought out strategy is required for a visit to the most sprawling museum in the world. After all, there is much more to admire in the Louvre than just the awe-inspiring ladies *Venus of Milo* (2nd century BC), Leonardo da Vinci's *Mona Lisa* (16th century) and Jan Vermeer's *The Lacemaker* (17th century). To avoid the long queue at the entrance under the pyramid, enter the INSIDERTIP ▶ *Porte des Lions (opened irregularly, ask in advance | tel. 01 40 20 53 17)* located in the Denon Wing on the Seine side. From there, you'll soon be standing in front of the perennially besieged *La Joconde*, the *Mona Lisa*, who shines in a new light in the recently renovated *Salle des Etats*.

You should also obtain a floor plan from the *Information counter* and the plan showing which collections are closed that week.

Culture seekers can then choose from a comprehensive range of exhibits dating back to the 7th century B.C. that includes Oriental, Egyptian (particularly monumental) and Graeco-Roman civilisations divided among the three building complexes *(Denon, Sully and Richelieu)*. Alongside European sculpture from the Middle Ages to the 19th century, handicrafts and over 100,000 graphic art pieces spanning six centuries, the collection of paintings is quite a highlight. Sub-divided into regions, it documents European

The park Jardin des Tuileries designed by André Le Nôtre is a World Heritage Site today

painting from the 13th to the 19th centuries. The exuberant stucco, the crown jewels and paintings by Charles Le Brun, Eugène Delacroix and others in the opulent *Apollon-Galerie* bear witness to the immense power of the Sun King, Louis XIV.

Take a break from your museum visit in the aesthetic underground shopping arcade, *Carrousel du Louvre*. Even if you forego a visit to the museum, it is still worthwhile to take a closer look at the Louvre complex, which was transformed from a 12th-century fortress into a Renaissance palace. The exposed *medieval foundations*, the beautifully illuminated *Cour Carée,* the small *triumphal arch* that forms a focal axis with its big brother and the audacious *glass pyramid* by the Chinese architect Ieoh Ming Pei are absolute highlights of any visit to Paris. The *Hall Napoléon* (admission 13 euros) in the lobby below the Pyramid hosts special exhibitions. Advance tickets are sold at railway stations (SNCF) or at Fnac: *tel. 08 92 68 46 94,* or from abroad: *tel. 0033 1 40 20 53 17.* The automatic ticket machines are easy to use.

Wed–Mon 9am–6pm (Wed and Fri until 10pm) | admission 12 euros (free up to 25 years) | M 1, 7 Palais Royal-Musée du Louvre | www.louvre.fr.

▇8▇ MUSÉE DE L'ORANGERIE
(146 A4) (*Ⓜ J7*)

The Jardin des Tuileries adjacent to the Louvre is home to the remarkable collection assembled by the art dealer Paul Guillaume, including works by Auguste Renoir, Pablo Picasso, Paul Cézanne, Henri Matisse and Amedeo Modigliani. The highlight is the famous *Nymphéas* (Water Lilies) by Claude Monet, whose eight large compositions adorn the walls in an elliptical form, enhancing the impression of flowing water and light.

A combined ticket with the Musée d'Orsay (14 euros) ensures priority in both queues. *Wed–Mon 9am–6pm | admission 9 euros | Place de la Concorde | Jardin des Tuileries | 1st arr. | M 1, 8, 12 Concorde | www.musee-orangerie.fr*

RELAX & ENJOY

Check out the *Bar à Sieste – Zzz-Zen* **(146 C3)** *(Ⓜ K6)* (*Mon–Sat noon–8pm | 29, Passage Choiseul | 2nd arr. | tel. 01 71 60 81 55 | M 7, 14 Pyramides | www.barsieste.com)* in the nostalgic Choiseul shopping centre. Without having to book ahead, you can relax on a Shiatsu massage lounger or chair and listen to ethereal music played through your headphones. The loungers are separated from each other by either walls or curtains. The most sophisticated Japanese devices knead and massage for 25 to 45 minutes, depending on the programme you select. Prices range between 12 and 27 euros, which is not very much by Paris standards.

A cup of organic tea is included. For a bit more pampering, head to the vaulted cellar for a fish pedicure (20 euros) or treat yourself to a manicure (from 12 euros).

Great art in an old railway station: sculptures in the central area of the Musée d'Orsay

▣ MUSÉE D'ORSAY ★ ●
(146 A–B 4–5) *(øʃ J7)*

The painters of light, the Impressionists, form the focal point in the rooms of this former railway station that was converted in 1986. Works by the precursors of modernist painting such as Vincent van Gogh, Paul Gauguin and Paul Cézanne can also be admired. The paintings, sculptures, collection of art objects as well as urban planning documentation, film and film poster art cover the period from 1848–1914, one of the most fruitful epochs in art history. Not only is the museum book shop's extensive selection impressive, but so is the elegant restaurant, where the modern seating harmonises well with the splendour of the Belle-Époque era. *Tue–Sun 9:30am–6pm (Thu until 9:45pm) | admission 11 euros | 1, rue de la Légion d'Honneur | 7th arr. | M Musée d'Orsay | RER C | www.musee-orsay.fr*

▣ PLACE DE LA CONCORDE
(146 A3) *(øʃ J6–7)*

The most monumental square in Paris is superlative in every way: you have the entire Champs-Elysées up to the Arc de Triomphe before your very eyes from its middle point, the 3,300 year-old, 22 m high (75 ft) Egyptian obelisk. It is hard to imagine that, on this very square built in 1775, thousands of opponents of the Revolution – including Louis XVI himself and his wife, Marie-Antoinette, Robespierre and the Countess du Barry, met their deaths here by guillotine. The eight female statues framing the Place de la Concorde represent the eight largest cities in France. *8th arr. | M 1, 8, 12 Concorde*

■11 PONT ALEXANDRE III
(145 E4) *(𝄞 H7)*

Tsar Nicholas II personally laid the foundation for the city's most magnificent bridge in 1896, which connects the Grand Palais and the Esplanade des Invalides. In sunny weather the gold of the winged Belle-Époque horses shimmering on the bridge's corner pillars can be seen from far and wide. *8th arr. | M 8, 13 Invalides / RER C Invalides*

SENTIER DISTRICT AND OPÉRA

The former Parisian cloth manufacturing district around the rue du Sentier is still the centre of haute couture today, but on a smaller scale.

The pressure caused by cheaper imports from Asia has caused a number of businesses to close and even the wholesale trade is suffering from competition from other regions. The chic Place des Victoires with boutiques and its architecturally stunning shopping arcades from the 19th century are a testimony to the former affluence of this district. You could easily spend half a day strolling through the covered shopping centres resplendent

The Pont Alexandre III is only one of 35 bridges over the Seine in Paris, but one of the prettiest

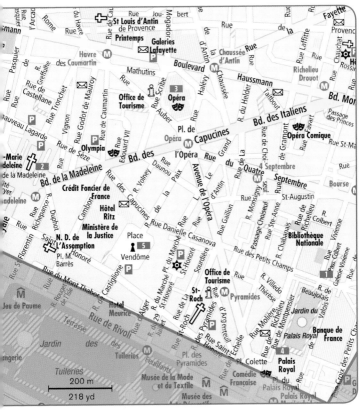

SIGHTSEEING IN THE SENTIER DISTRICT

▨▨▨ Pedestrian precinct

1 Galerie Vivienne
2 La Madeleine
3 Opéra Garnier
4 Palais Royal & Jardin du Palais Royal
5 Place Vendôme

with mirrors, brass and wooden panelling, where you feel as if you have travelled back in time to the elegant 18th century (albeit slightly faded), complete with stagecoaches on the streets. The area between the Palais Royal and the Boulevard Montmartre is lined with some better and some less-well restored arcades, ideal for those looking for old books and handicrafts, or who enjoy shopping in exquisite, time-honoured shops. Afterwards, enjoy a break in one of the area's quiet, stylish cafés. The famous department stores, Galeries Lafayette and Printemps, are also in the vicinity.

In this district of Paris a large amount of money is spent as well as earned.

The Opéra Garnier was the largest opera house in the world when it was constructed in 1875

Apart from the imposing headquarters of major banks and insurance agencies there is also the classical building that houses the Paris stock exchange, although there has long been no floor trading here. The street cafés and restaurants are frequented by elegantly-clad business people holding extended lunch meetings. The Opéra Garnier lends the district its share of culture. A little further north, the legendary artistic and entertainment district of Montmartre stretches up the hill (see *Discovery Tour 2*).

■ GALERIE VIVIENNE ●
(146 C3) (*∅ L6*)

The gallery is considered the queen of Parisian arcades and was completely refurbished at the turn of the millennium. Here, under glass-domed roofs, you can saunter past select shops over the beautiful mosaics on the floor made in the neo-Classical style. After a visit to *Emilio Robba,* where you'll find the most gorgeous artificial flowers, sample an exquisite *chocolat à l'ancienne* in the tea room, *A priori thé*. Not far afield is the building of the same vintage, the *Galerie Colbert* with its Pompeian-style rotunda. *4, rue des Petits Champs | 2nd arr. | M 3 Bourse*

☑ LA MADELEINE
(146 A2) (*ᗿ J6*)

The church *Sainte-Marie Madeleine,* built in 1764 and reminiscent of a Greek temple, was used by Napoleon as a monument to the glory of his army. It later served as a parliament building, stock exchange and national library. It was first consecrated as a church in 1842. Today, it is a venue for memorial services for famous singers and actors. *Daily 7:30am–7pm | Place de la Madeleine | 8th arr. | M 8, 12, 14 Madeleine*

☑ OPÉRA GARNIER
(146 B2) (*ᗿ K5*)

The sumptuous palace laden with marble and gold was completed by Charles Garnier in 1875 and can be visited outside rehearsal hours. The opulent vestibule is quite remarkable, as are the ceiling paintings created by Marc Chagall in 1964. *Daily 10am–6pm | 10 euros | Place de l'Opéra | 9th arr. | M 3, 7, 8 Opéra | RER A Auber | www.operadeparis.fr*

☑ PALAIS ROYAL & JARDIN DU
PALAIS ROYAL (146 C3–4) (*ᗿ K–L 6–7*)

A historic place of refuge in the turbulent city centre. Shaded by the lime trees, it was once an epicentre of historical significance. Cardinal Richelieu, who had the palace and its surrounding park constructed in 1634, later bequeathed it to Louis XIII. Its subsequent owners, the House of Orléans, expanded it. Behind the uniform façades with rounded, arched arcades, shops can still be found just like centuries ago. The French Revolution began here in July 1789. In the adjacent courtyard next to the *Comédie Française,* the columns of varying heights by Daniel Buren have provided an interesting counterbalance to the historical backdrop since 1986. *1st arr. | M 1, 7 Palais Royal-Musée du Louvre*

☑ PLACE VENDÔME
(146 B3) (*ᗿ J–K6*)

This masterpiece of classical symmetry with its characteristic oblique square form on four sides was built at the end of the 17th century by the famous master builder Jules Hardouin-Mansart. A column in the style of a Roman Trojan column stands in the middle of the Place Vendôme, and at its crown Napoleon is depicted as a Roman emperor. Place Vendôme is also world-wide known for its renowned jewellers and the famous Hôtel Ritz, which benefits from the location's extraordinary atmosphere. *1st arr. | M 3, 7, 8 Opéra*

KEEP FIT!

The lovely *Parc des Buttes-Chaumont* (see p. 57) on the eastern side of the city with its bridges, pavilions and waterfalls is definitely worth the 15-minute Métro ride. And, if you want to do something to keep fit, arrive shortly before 9am for the free hour-long Qigong course offered by Maître Thoi, a master of this popular Chinese sport said to strengthen inner energy. For over 22 years, Thoi has held his class 365 days a year, regardless of the weather, at Av. de la Cascade **(143 E5)** (*ᗿ Q4*) across from Rosa Bonheur *(M 7bis Botzaris).*

FROM LES HALLES TO THE BASTILLE

The shopping centre Les Halles, built on the site of the former indoor markets known as the "belly of Paris" (Emile Zola), and now surrounded by budget outlets of all sorts, is only a stone's throw from the former aristocratic district of Marais.

This district begins right behind the world renowned cultural centre, the Centre Georges Pompidou. Many Jews have lived in this area since the beginning of the 12th century. The Shoah Memorial (*www.memorialdelashoha.org*) as well as a Jewish museum of art and history (*www.mahj.org*) are both located in Marais and document the Jews' turbulent fate in France. On Friday evenings there is always a hub of activity between the kosher shops and the few remaining synagogues. "Pletzl" on the rue des Rosiers has long been a gathering place for Jews from throughout Europe. Its small shops and restaurants are increasingly being replaced by trendy, upmarket stores.

Marais is not only a fashionable district but also the quartier of the gay community. Stores for men's cosmetics are interspersed with fancy women's clothing stores, jewellers, galleries and cafés where there is always something going on. The district's architecture is imposing with its many aristocratic residences, some of which house museums today. The Place des Vosges, a former royal square, is one of the most beautiful in Paris. Buskers play here year round. The centre of Paris' nightlife, just a short walk to the east of here, pulsates with activity until early morning in the shadow of the Opéra Bastille, around the rue

An artistic event both inside and out: the Centre Georges Pompidou

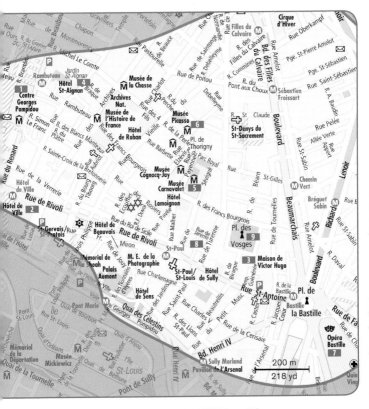

SIGHTSEEING BETWEEN LES HALLES AND BASTILLE

1 Centre Pompidou

2 Hôtel de Ville & Place de
l'Hôtel de Ville

3 Maison de Victor Hugo

4 Musée d'Art et d'Histoire du
Judaïsme

5 Musée Carnavalet

6 Musée Picasso

7 Opéra Bastille

8 Place du Marché Sainte-
Cathérine

9 Place des Vosges

⬙ Pedestrian precinct

du Faubourg Saint-Antoine, as well as further north in the vicinity of the rue Oberkampf.

1 CENTRE POMPIDOU ★
(147 E4) (*Ø M7*)

The fourth and fifth levels of this futuristic tubular structure give you a comprehensive overview of 20th-century art. The interdisciplinary approach to graphic art, architecture, design and new media is fascinating. A true-to-life replica of the studio of the famous sculptor Constantin Brancusi is situated on the forecourt outside the building. ☼ On the sixth level, temporary exhibits of works by world renowned artists are displayed. The phenomenal view of Paris alone is worth a visit, which you can also admire from the designer café *Le George*. Next to the Centre is the fountain comprising water spraying sculptures by Niki de Saint Phalle and Jean Tinguely in a tribute to the ballet Le Sacre du Printemps by Igor Stravinsky, characterised by its colourful figures and technical contraptions – a meeting place for the younger crowd. *Wed–Mon 11am–9pm (Thu until 11pm, Atelier Brancusi 2pm–6pm) | admission 13 euros, observation deck 3 euros | Place Georges-Pompidou | 4th arr. | M 11 Rambuteau | www.centre pompidou.fr*

▣ HÔTEL DE VILLE & PLACE DE L'HÔTEL DE VILLE
(147 E5) (*ℳ M8*)

After an incendiary attack in 1882, the city hall was rebuilt in the Renaissance Revival style. Its façade features sculptures of over one hundred Parisian personalities. During the Middle Ages, the formerly centrally located square in front of the building extended to the jetty of the Seine. At one time it was a venue for folk festivals and executions; today, by contrast, demonstrations are held here and it is also the site of a floodlit artificial skating rink in winter. *Mon–Fri 8:30am–5pm | free admission | tel. registration required: 01 42 76 40 40 | 4th arr. | M 1, 11 Hôtel de Ville*

▣ MAISON VICTOR HUGO
(148 B6) (*ℳ O8*)

The writer Victor Hugo lived and worked here between 1832 and 1848. Some of the ☾ rooms have an Asian influence. Here, you not only have a wonderful view of the Place des Vosges, but you can also marvel at the poet's documents, objects and paintings, which reveal he was also a very good painter – he left numerous paintings and around 3,000 drawings. *Tue–Sun 10am–6pm | free admission | 6, pl. des Vosges | 4th arr. | M 1 Saint-Paul | www.maisonsvictorhugo.paris.fr*

The colourful Stravinsky fountain by Niki de Saint Phalle and Jean Tinguely

Bastille: a venue where people now storm in for the opera

4 MUSÉE D'ART ET D'HISTOIRE DU JUDAISME (147 F4) (*M7*)

Situated at the centre of the Jewish quarter in Paris, this museum recounts the history of the Jewish community in Europe – particular in France – by means of numerous documents and handcrafted objects from the Middle Ages up to the 20th century, as well as archives documenting the Dreyfus Affair. *Mon–Fri 11am–6pm, Sun 10am–6pm | admission 8 euros | 71, rue du Temple | 3rd arr. | M 1 Hôtel de Ville | M 11 Rambuteau | www. mahj.org*

5 MUSÉE CARNAVALET ● (148 A5) (*N8*)

In the opulent city palace dating back to 1548, only a few feet from the Place des Vosges, the tumultuous history of Paris from Roman times until today unfolds. A model shows the huge incissions made by Baron Haussmann into the urban fabric. Numerous paintings as well as objects (i.e. garments worn by revolutionaries and models of the guillotine) document milestones in the city's development. The museum also has temporary exhibitions. *Tue–Sun 10am–6pm | free admission | 16, rue des Francs-Bourgeois | 4th arr. | M 1 Saint-Paul | www.carnavalet.paris.fr*

6 MUSÉE PICASSO ★ (148 A5) (*N7*)

Some art aficianados claim that Pablo Picasso (1881–1973) was the greatest artist o fthe 20th century. The Picasso museum in Marais holds the largest collection of his works with 5,000 pieces. After having closed for five years of renovations, the exhibition space has been expanded to over 39,000 square feet. Make sure to take a look at the artist's private collection with works by Henri Matisse, Edgar Degas and others. You will need plenty of time for this first rate museum and the stately *Hôtel Salé* in which it is housed. *Tue–Sun 11:30am–6pm (3x Fri per month until 9pm) | admission 11 euros | 8, rue de Thorigny | 3rd arr. | M 8 Saint-Sébastien-Froissart | www. museepicassoparis.fr*

7 OPÉRA BASTILLE (154 B1) (*O9*)

The silvery façade of glass, steel and granite on the Place de la Bastille is hard to miss. The former President François Mitterrand commissioned the Canadian architect Carlos Ott to construct a new opera house which was completed in 1989. Even if you do not want to attend any of the opera or ballet performances, it is still worth the 1½-hour tour. *Mon–Fri, book ahead: tel. 01 40 01 19 70 | admission 12 euros | 120, rue de Lyon | 12th arr. | M 1, 5, 8 Bastille | www.operadeparis.fr*

🔲 PLACE DU MARCHÉ SAINTE-CATHÉRINE (148 A5–6) (*ⅅⅅ N8*)

The cafés and shady trees of this quiet location in Marais will carry you off to a tranquil marketplace in a provincial town in the South of France, especially in summer. *4th arr. | M 1 Saint-Paul*

Place des Vosges: fountains at the centre of a harmonious ensemble

🔲 PLACE DES VOSGES ⭐ (148 A–B 5–6) (*ⅅⅅ N–O8*)

At the beginning of the 17th century, King Henry IV commissioned the construction of the *Place Royale*. It is not only one of the oldest, but also one of the most architecturally harmonious squares in the city. The 36 pavilions (those for the king and queen are slightly higher) are framed by arcades where elegant art galleries and restaurants are now housed. Above these, the symmetrically arranged façades with their composition of light natural stone, red brick facing and grey slated roofs create a perfect picture. The uniformity of the ensemble is best appreciated from the small park situated in the centre of the square. *4th arr. | M 1 Saint-Paul, M 1, 5, 8 Bastille*

RIVE GAUCHE AND THE ISLANDS

The ⭐ *Île de la Cité* is the heart of Paris. The first inhabitants, the Parisii, settled here during the Roman era.
This is also where the Gothic architectural masterpiece, the Cathédrale de Notre-Dame, is located. The fortified towers of the Conciergerie and the wonderfully light Sainte-Chapelle round off the medieval appearance of this vibrant area. On the neighbouring *Île Saint-Louis,* the pace is slightly more relaxed. This small island, which was long uninhabited, is now the most prestigious areas of Paris. The most lively street by far is the rue St-Louis, which has more ice cream shops than anywhere else in the city. In the summer, queues form from one to the next. The best place to enjoy your ice cream, however, is on the Pont Saint

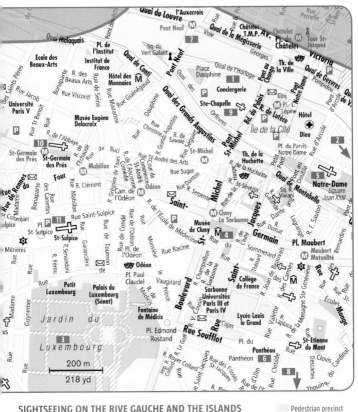

SIGHTSEEING ON THE RIVE GAUCHE AND THE ISLANDS

▨ Pedestrian precinct

- **1** Conciergerie
- **2** Institut du Monde Arabe
- **3** Jardin du Luxembourg
- **4** Musée de Cluny
- **5** Notre-Dame
- **6** Panthéon
- **7** Pont Neuf
- **8** Rue Mouffetard
- **9** Sainte-Chapelle
- **10** Saint-Germain-des-Prés
- **11** Saint-Sulpice

Louis, which connects both islands and where INSIDER TIP street musicians give their finest performances.

While the *rive droite* is traditionally more bourgeois, the Quartier Latin and Saint-Germain-des-Prés on the left bank of the Seine, the *rive gauche,* have long been the centres of intellectual life. Existentialists congregated in cafés in the 1950s. Today these areas are frequented predominantly by tourists and employees of the surrounding publishing houses and booksellers. The Quarter Latin (where Latin was once spoken) has housed the most famous educational institutions of the nation since the 13th century. In addition, the area has cafés and bistros as well as one of the most

More relevant than ever: the Institut du Monde Arabe

popular parks in Paris, the Jardin du Luxembourg.

■1 CONCIERGERIE (147 D5–6) (⌀ *L8*)

The "antechamber to the guillotine" – as this former prison is rather grimly known – is an imposing structure on the Île de la Cité that chronicles a tragic episode in French history. The most prominent among the more than 2,000 inmates who faced their execution here were Marie Antoinette (her cell has now been reconstructed) as well as the revolutionaries Georges Danton and Maximilien de Robespierre. The picturesque building with its rounded towers was originally a palace of the Capetian ruling dynasty from the 10th century. The *Salle des Gens d'Armes* is considered one of the most impressive examples of Gothic secular architecture. Its name is derived from the word *concierge*, or chamberlain, who was accorded great power by the king from around 1300 onwards. *Daily 9:30am–6pm | 9.50 euros (incl. Sainte-Chapelle 13.50 euros) | 1, quai de l'Horloge | 1st arr. | www.conciergerie. monuments-nationaux.fr*

■2 INSTITUT DU MONDE ARABE (153 F2) (⌀ *N9*)

The striking glass and aluminium façades, a successful paradigm of modern architecture by Jean Nouvel, follows the curve of the Seine. A gimmicky feature of the institute are the photography slats on the south side which open and close according to the fall of light. To promote the cultural exchange between the European and Islamic world, 20 Arab nations present forums, films and exhibitions, and there is also an extensive library. ☆ The restaurant, *Le Ziryab*, provides a spectacular view over the roofs of the metropolis. *Tue–Sun 10am–6pm | admission 8 euros | 1, rue des Fossés Saint-Bernard | 5th arr. | M 7, 10 Jussieu | www. imarabe.org*

■3 JARDIN DU LUXEMBOURG ★ ● (152 B–C2) (⌀ *K–L 9–10*)

The most famous park in the centre of Paris is quite close to the Sorbonne. You can watch children sailing boats in the large pond from one of the available chairs. Maria de' Medici had the park and palace constructed at the beginning of the 17th century as an imitation of her native Florence. The *Palais du Luxembourg* is the headquarters of the French Senate today. The adjacent *Musée du Luxembourg* often has exceptional exhibitions. *Park: in summer 7am until 1 hour before sunset, in winter from 8am | 6th arr. | M Luxembourg | RER B*

◾ MUSÉE DE CLUNY (153 D1) *(📖 L9)*
The late Gothic city palace of the abbots of Cluny next to the Roman spas from the 3rd century provides the ideal setting for this display of medieval art. Apart from illuminated manuscripts, furniture, crafted pieces and ancient sculptures, the stained-glass windows and wall tapestries are especially stunning. The round salon featuring six wall tapestries of the INSIDER TIP *Lady with the Unicorn* (15th century) is a highlight. While the first five tapestries are allegories of the five senses, the meaning of the sixth is a mystery which holds every visitor under its spell. *Wed–Mon 9:15am–5:45pm |* *admission 8 euros | 6, pl. Paul Painlevé | 5th arr. | M 10 Cluny-La Sorbonne | www. musee-moyenage.fr*

◾ NOTRE-DAME ⭐ (147 E6) *(📖 M9)*
This Gothic masterpiece was built between 1163 and 1345 at the instigation of Bishop Maurice de Sully. A Roman temple once stood on the square 2,000 years before. The interior of the five-aisled nave can accommodate 9,000 people. The three large entrance portals, the massive buttresses around the choir and the rose windows with a diameter of over 32 feet are especially impressive.

BOOKS & FILMS

A Moveable Feast – Ernest Hemingway describes his sojourn in Paris during the Roaring Twenties. Follow his footsteps to restaurants such as *Closerie des Lilas*

Midnight in Paris – Woody Allen's Oscar-winning film of 2012 borrowed all the clichés about Paris. Its beautiful pictures of the city in various classic periods in history play into the hands of the Paris tourist office

The Greater Journey: Americans in Paris – David McCollough's story of adventurous American artists, writers, doctors, politicians, architects, and others of high aspiration who set off for Paris between 1830 and 1900, ambitious to excel in their work, is both enthralling and inspiring

Hotel du Nord – The classic work of poetic Realism by Marcel Carné (1938) takes place on the Canal Saint-Martin, which has once again become trendy

The Sweet Life in Paris – American pastry chef David Lebovitz recounts his adventures as a new resident in Paris – complete with 50 original recipes

Ratatouille – The highly acclaimed animated film by Brad Bird about a rat turned cooking genius who took the culinary world by storm was awarded an Oscar in 2008

La Vie en Rose – Marion Cotillard won an Oscar for her performance in this portrayal of the tragic life of Edith Piaf directed by Oliver Dahan in 2007.

Paris, je t'aime – 21 renowned filmmakers made a declaration of love to the city in 2006 with 18 short films that play in just as many arondissements

Notre-Dame: mythical creatures as figurative decoration high above the cathedral tower

Many historically significant events have taken place here, including Napoleon's coronation. During the revolution, Notre-Dame was transformed into a "Temple of Reason" and the church seemed to be in danger of demise. In his book *The Hunchback of Notre-Dame*, Victor Hugo successfully appealed to the public to stop tolerating the situation, and the cathedral was restored as a result.

The ☀ tower provides a good view of the gargoyles as well as the city. In the forecourt there is a special marking from which distances to other French cities can be measured. *Mon–Fri 8am–6:45pm, Sat/Sun 8am–7:15pm | free admission | tower: April–Sept daily 10am–6:30pm, Oct–March daily 10am–5:30pm | 8.50 euros (Oct–March free admission on the first Sunday of the month) | Parvis Notre-Dame-Place Jean-Paul II | Île de la Cité | 4th arr. | M 4 Cité or St-Michel | RER B, C Saint-Michel/Notre-Dame | www.notredamedeparis.fr*

6 PANTHÉON

(153 D2) (*ℳ L10*)

This massive domed structure can be seen from a distance on the hill of Sainte-Geneviève. Louis XV had the edifice constructed in 1756 by his master builder Jacques-Germain Soufflot as the fulfillment of a vow to Geneviève, the patron saint of Paris. Shortly after the Revolution, the church became the final resting place of French luminaries such as Voltaire and Jean-Jacques Rousseau. Since Victor Hugo's body was transferred to the Panthéon in 1885, this building – that is still occasionally used as a place of worship – was finally considered a mausoleum. You can also scale the stairs to the ☀ gallery of the dome from which the physicist Léon Foucault conducted his famous pendulum experiment demonstrating the earth's rotational axis. *April–Sept daily 10am–6:30pm, Oct–March daily 10am–6pm | 8.50 euros (Oct–March free the first Sunday of the month) | Place du Panthéon |*

5th arr. | M 10 Cardinal Lemoine | RER B Luxembourg | www.pantheon.monuments-nationaux.fr

⑦ PONT NEUF
(147 D5) *(ψ L8)*

The "new" bridge that crosses the top of the Île de la Cité is in fact the city's oldest existing bridge. When Henry IV, whose equestrian statue stands atop the structure, inaugurated the bridge in 1607, it was considered highly modern. For the first time in Paris, the view from a bridge of the Seine was unobstructed. It is the most famous crossing point on the Seine – often sung about, the object of countless paintings and the backdrop for many films. The ⚡ INSIDER TIP square beneath the equestrian statue provides a magnificent view of the Louvre. *1st/6th arr. | M 7 Pont Neuf*

⑧ RUE MOUFFETARD
(153 E2–4) *(ψ M10–11)*

This little street has wound its way down the vibrant Montagne Sainte-Geneviève since Roman times. Students from schools in the area, tourists and locals treasure the narrow street with its daily, well-stocked markets at the lower end as well as its small bars and boutiques. The scenic *Place de la Contrescarp* with its lovely cafés is located at the upper end of the "Mouff". *5th arr. | M 7 Place Monge*

⑨ SAINTE-CHAPELLE
(147 D6) *(ψ L8)*

This veritable treasure chest of Gothic architecture lies virtually hidden in the courtyard of the central law courts on the Île de la Cité. The 13th-century church houses valuable relics from the Holy Land. The effect of the massive stained glass windows reaching for the heavens, held together only by filigree buttresses that bathe the entire room in a pale blue light is breathtaking. The upper floor is the actual chapel and was reserved for the king. *March–Oct daily 9:30am–6pm, Nov–Feb daily 9am–5pm | admission 8.50 euros (incl. Conciergerie 13.50 euros) | 4, bd. du Palais | 1st arr. | M 4 Saint-Michel, Cité | www.sainte-chapelle.monuments-nationaux.fr*

⑩ SAINT-GERMAIN-DES-PRÉS
(146 C6) *(ψ K8)*

Though the church is a part of the once powerful Benedictine abbey from the 8th century, only the bell tower remains. The Bible was translated into French for the first time here, and it is the final resting place of the philosopher René Descartes. *Mon 12:30pm–7:45pm, Tue–Sun 8am–7:45pm | 3, pl. Saint-Germain-des-Prés | 6th arr. | M 4 Saint-Germain-des-Prés*

⑪ SAINT-SULPICE
(152 C1) *(ψ K9)*

This 17th-century church with its two elegant rows of pillars is situated on a lively square with a Roman fountain. The paintings by Eugène Delacroix in the first chapel on the right are equally remarkable. *Daily 8am–7:30pm | 2, rue Palatine | 6th arr. | M 4 Saint-Sulpice*

OTHER DISTRICTS

BELLEVILLE
(148–149 C–D 1–2) *(ψ P–Q 5–6)*

In contrast to the affluent western part of the city, the Belleville district has retained its more modest character to a large extent. Workers, clerks and immigrants predominantly live here. The district has an authentic neighbourly feeling

The east entrance of the National Library

impressive upon first glance, the "Très Grande Bibliothèque", completed in 1996, has numerous operational flaws, not least of which is that the books stored in the glass towers were exposed to too much sunlight, necessitating an incredibly expensive Venetian blind system. *Tue–Sat 10am–7pm, Sun 1pm–7pm | admission 3.50 euros, special exhibits 7 euros | 11 quai François Mauriac | 13th arr. | M 14 | RER C Bibliothèque François Mitterrand | www.bnf.fr*

BOIS DE BOULOGNE
(136–137 B–E6) (*ⓂA–D 4–9*)

The large green lung to the west of Paris covering an area of over 3 square miles was the fashionable recreational meeting place at the beginning of the 20th century. The many hiking, riding and bicycle trails as well as small lakes, two horse-racing tracks and diverse restaurants are located in the park and its forests that have sadly been dissected by the many surrounding roads. In the 18th century, the nobility built small summer residences. One of the most popular is the small castle of Bagatelle in the *Parc de Bagatelle (admission 5.50 euros)*, which is beautifully manicured and intersected by streams. The rose garden is a delight for flower lovers.

The nearby *Jardin d'Acclimatation (admission 3 euros)* is a children's paradise (*see p. 118*) without over-hyped attractions and is also fun for grown-ups. There are two bicycle rental agencies and rowing boats for hire at the *Lac Inférieur. M 1 Les Sablons*

without the tourists, particularly the Musette area where Edith Piaf grew up; the small *Musée Edith Piaf (Mon–Wed 1pm–6pm, Thu 10am–noon / only after prebooking by phone: tel. 0143555272 | free admission | 5, rue Crespin du Gast)* displays various aspects of her life. Ever since artists discovered the charm and relatively low prices of the area, Bellevue has also become fashionable. Enjoy a beautiful view over Paris and the alleyways winding up the incline of ☆ Belvedere from the upper half of Bellevue park. *20th arr. | M 2, 11 Belleville*

BIBLIOTHÈQUE NATIONALE DE FRANCE
(154 C5) (*ⓂP12*)

A Grand Projet by the architect Dominique Perrault from the Mitterrand era: a quartet of massive high-rises in the form of open books surrounding a small grove. Although aesthetically

LES CATACOMBES ●
(152 B5) (*ⓂK12*)

Stone was extracted from underground quarries and used for Paris' buildings. The over 185-mile-long network of passageways, which some Parisians use for illegal parties, is partially open for tours. Since Parisian cemeteries were overcrowded until the 18th century, the bones of previous generations were decoratively piled up in these catacombs. *Tue–Sun 10am–8pm, last admission 7pm | 8 euros | start of tour: 1, pl. Denfert-Rochereau | 14th arr. | M 4, 6 | RER B Denfert-Rochereau | www.catacombes.paris.fr*

CIMETIÈRE DE MONTMARTRE
(140 B3–4) (*M J–K3*)

A number of artists and literati including Hector Berlioz, Heinrich Heine, Alexandre Dumas, Edgar Degas, Jacques Offenbach, François Truffaut, Vaslav Nijinsky, Emile Zola and Stendhal found their final resting place in this picturesque cemetery. *Daily 8am–5:30pm | 20, av. Rachel | 18th arr. | M 2 Blanche | M 13 La Fourche*

CIMETIÈRE DU PÈRE LACHAISE ●
(149 E–F 4–5) (*M Q–R 7–8*)

With an area of 110 acres, 12,000 trees, 1.5 million graves and ostentatious tombs, this cemetery is certainly the largest and most spectacular in Paris. In particular, the graves of the *Doors* lead singer Jim Morrison as well as Edith Piaf attract a huge following. Yves Montand, Baron Haussmann, Honoré de Balzac, Marcel Proust, Oscar Wilde, Frédéric Chopin and Molière are also buried here. *Daily 8:30am–5pm | 16, rue du Repos | 20th arr. | M 2, 3 Père Lachaise*

FONDATION LOUIS VUITTON
(136 C6) (*M B5*)

Since the end of 2014, a huge futuristic glass cloud designed by the famous architect Frank Gehry has graced the eastern part of Bois de Boulogne. The building with its galleries ranging in height

Very imaginatively designed tombs in the Père Lachaise cemetery

from 11 m (36 ft) to 21 m (69 ft) is a masterpiece in itself. It houses recent pieces by internationally renowned artists, including Gerhard Richter, Jeff Koons and Olafur Eliasson. Temporary exhibitions as well as contemporary music concerts round out the offerings. *Mon, Wed, Thu noon–7pm, Fri noon–11pm, Sat/Sun 11am–8pm | admission 14 euros | 8, av. du Mahatma Gandhi | M1 Le Sablons | www.fondationlouisvuitton.fr*

by great artists and still used for artistic purposes today. Renowned artists such as Pablo Picasso, Amedeo Modigliani, Marc Chagall and Henri Matisse worked in the *Chemin du Montparnasse* on the Avenue du Maine after World War I. The places they frequented, namely La Coupole, Closerie des Lilas, Le Dôme or La Rotonde, are still favourite meeting places. Lenin und Leo Trotsky held political meetings in La Rotonde that were regularly interrupted by the police. Prominent literary

Schon das Gebäude ist ein avantgardistisches Kunstwerk: Fondation Louis Vuitton

MONTPARNASSE
(152 A–B 3–4) (ᗰ J–K 10–12)

The *Tour Montparnasse (April–Sept daily 9:30am–11:30pm | Oct–March 9:30am–11pm | 14.50 euros | www.tourmontparnasse56.com)* skyscraper that towers above everything else can only really be appreciated when standing on its ⚡ viewing platform, the highest in Paris. When you wander through this district, you will find ugly buildings constructed in the 1960s alongside idyllic, green courtyards and studios onced used

figures such as Samuel Beckett, Charles Baudelaire, Jean-Paul Sartre and Simone de Beauvoir are buried at the *Cimetière du Montparnasse*. *19th arr. | M 4, 6, 12, 13 Montparnasse-Bienvenüe | M 6 Edgar Quinet*

INSIDER TIP MUSÉE MARMOTTAN
(158 C4) (ᗰ C7)

The painting that gave Impressionism its name, *Impression Soleil Levant*, hangs next to a hundred other masterpieces by Claude Monet (1840–1926) on the lower level of the opulent villa near the Bois de Boulogne. Precious biblical paintings as well as paintings from Monet's private collection (including works by Edgar Degas, Edouard Manet and Auguste Renoir) hang in the upper living area. A must for every lover of Impressionist art! *Tue–Sun 10am–6pm (Thu until 8pm) | admission 11 euros | 2, rue Louis Boilly | 16th arr. | M 9 La Muette | www.marmottan.fr*

PARC DES BUTTES-CHAUMONT 🔆
(142–143 C–E 5–6) *(ⓜ P–Q 4–5)*

In the 19th century, Napoleon III had a picturesque landscaped park laid out in the English style with grottoes, rock formations, valleys, shrines and waterfalls on a waste tip in the then-notorious eastern part of Paris. With the help of the most modern technology of the day and numerous explosives, the terraced grounds were created to a variety of different designs – including one with a lake and an island – and planted with unusual vegetation. *19th arr. | M 7b Buttes-Chaumont*

PLACE DU TERTRE
(141 D4) *(ⓜ L3)*

There is hardly a trace of the former village-like calm here. Instead, the area has been taken over by droves of tourists clamouring for their portrait rendered by artists of varying talent. The cafés that border the square are ideal for reminiscing about the era when luminaries still whiled away their time here. *M 12 Abesses*

SACRÉ-CŒUR
(141 D4) *(ⓜ L3)*

The dazzling white basilica rising high above the city on Montmartre seems almost surreal, and cynics claim the domes look as if a confectioner has been having fun. The interior has a stunning giant golden Byzantine-style mosaic. The edifice was built as a national monument after France's defeat by Germany in the Franco-Prussian War of 1870. In 1919 the pilgrimage church was dedicated to the "Sacred Heart of Jesus". Today, thousands make the pilgrimage up the many steps and enjoy the impressive view over Paris from the ● 🔆 church's forecourt. A more comfortable option for making the ascent is a small mountain railway. *Daily 6am–11pm | 35, rue du Chevalier de la Barre | 8th arr. | M 2 Anvers*

OUTSIDE THE CITY

SAINT-DENIS
(158 C2) *(ⓜ 0)*

Stunning, early Gothic pillared basilica (started in 1135) which became the prototype for this architectural style in France. A visit to the *royal tombs* is one of the highlights of any tour of this church located in the Paris suburb Saint-Denis. For centuries, nearly every ruler of the nation was buried here. There are 75 monumental tombs in the crypt, each guarded by life-sized statues of the deceased. The first church was built on this site in the 5th century when the martyr Denis allegedly walked up Montmartre with his severed head. *Summer daily 10am–6pm, winter daily 10am–5pm | tombs: 8.50 euros | M 13 Basilique de Saint-Denis | www.saint-denis.monuments-nationaux.fr*

SAINT-GERMAIN-EN-LAYE
(158 A3) *(ⓜ 0)*

Excursions to the old royal city Saint-Germain-en-Laye were already popular among Parisians in the 19th century. This was not only on account of the convenient connection to the nation's first railway system which was constructed in 1837. French royalty resided in the town of 40,000 inhabitants until the end of the 17th century.

The landscape architects of Versailles laid out a beautiful *park* around the fortress-like, pentagonal *palace* with an over mile-long ⚜ *viewing platform* high above the Seine. Saint-Germain has retained the flair of a pleasant provincial town. The old town's streets and pedestrianised lanes with the beautiful palaces of the nobility and the large forest are ideal for a stroll and make an unforgettable outing. In addition, many shops are open on Sunday morning.

The *tourist office (38, rue Au-Pain | www. ot-saintgermainenlaye.fr)* is situated in the house where the composer Claude Debussy was born. The INSIDER TIP *studio of the Symbolist painter Maurice Denis* is worth a visit where works by Paul Gauguin and Pierre Bonnard are also exhibited. Saint-Germain-en-Laye is only 25 minutes away from Charles de Gaulle-Etoile via RER A.

VERSAILLES ★ (158 B4) (𝑀 0)

A Paris stay is not complete without a visit to Louis XIV's gigantic palace. There is virtually nowhere else where the power of the monarch is so resolute and impressive, yet tastefully and harmoniously implemented as in Versailles. The absolutist and centralist concept of a nation was personified by the "Sun King", Louis XIV (1638–1715). At his behest, nearly all of France's nobility resided here, which meant that as many as 20,000 people had to be provided for as well as entertained with lavish celebrations.

Absolute must-sees during the tour of the *palace (April–Oct Tue–Sun 9am– 6:30pm, Nov–March Tue–Sun 9am– 5:30pm | admission 15 euros, free for those under 26)* are the *royal chapel,* the *opéra* and the *state rooms* on the first floor, the walls of which are finished in marble and decorated with gold bro-

cade. Don't miss the 245-foot-long *Hall of Mirrors*, whose 17 windows cast light onto the mirrors opposite. Due to the lengthy queues, a morning or afternoon visit is recommended, the latter having the added advantage of reduced admission after 3pm.

Once measuring 23 square miles, this park *(April–Oct daily 7am–8:30 pm, Nov–March daily 8am–6pm | admission free, except March–Oct Sat/Sun 9 euros)* still covers an area of 2,000 acres. In addition to the pond where you can enjoy boat rides, its highlights inlcude the two smaller castles *Grand* and *Petit Trianon*. The newly designed *Domaine de Marie-Antoinette et Grand Trianon (April–Oct Tue–Sun noon–6:30pm, Nov–March Tue–Sun noon–5pm | admission 10 euros)* includes grottoes, a temple of love and streams in the pretty English garden as well as *Le Hameau,* the idealised replica of a village farm complete with a pond. If you prefer not to walk, you can cycle, take a tourist train or a boat ride. During the *Grandes Eaux Mu-* *sicales (April–Oct Sat/Sun several times a day; also Tue in June /July | 9 euros)* classical music provides the background for the water displays in the fountains of the park.

Complete "Passport Château Versailles" package 18.00 euros. Advanced tickets can also be obtained on the Internet: *www.chateau versailles.fr* and at *Fnac: tel. 08 92 68 46 94 | www.fnactickets.com* The easiest and quickest way to reach Versailles from Paris is on the suburban train RER C (Versailles-Rive Gauche), which takes around 30 minutes. It is only a short walk from the railway station. Trains to Versailles-Rive Droite (then bus marked Phébus) travel every 15 minutes from the Gare Saint-Lazare and from the Gare Montparnasse (direction Chartres) to Versailles-Chantier (then bus marked Phébus). Bus route 171 goes from the Métro station Pont de Sèvres (M 9) to the palace. Count on spending at least a day at Versailles and don't forget to wear comfortable shoes.

France's most famous palace and World Heritage Site: Versailles

FOOD & DRINK

To the French, eating is so much more than simply nourishment. It is also an essential means of social interaction and a vital ingredient in enhancing the quality of life.

If you want to discover the multifaceted gastronomy of France for yourself, which is well-represented in the top notch restaurants in the capital, you ought to know the fundamental aspects of French eating habits beforehand.

Breakfast *(petit déjeuner)* in France is modest by the standards of many other nations, but rightfully so: you'll need room for the much more substantial lunch *(déjeuner)*, that usually lasts for two hours and is only half as costly as dinner *(dîner)*.

Most restaurants do not open for dinner in the evening before 8pm. After an *apéritif* (kir, champagne or pastis) to wrap up your day, enjoy an *amuse-gueule* (a bite-sized starter) that will palatably match the meal ahead. You'll then be faced with the decision whether to order *à la carte* (from the menu) or *table d'hôte* (a set meal). With the former you have more selection, but will have to dig deeper into your pockets. Fortunately, people are no longer expected to opt for three or four courses, though it is customary to order a starter *(hors d'œuvre)* and a main course, or a main course and a dessert.

A set meal traditionally consists of an appetiser *(entrée)*, main course *(plat)* –

Photo: Senderens restaurant

Bon appétit: the majority of restaurants in Paris are temples of exquisite cuisine both at lunchtime and in the evening

usually meat *(viande)* or fish *(poisson)*, cheese *(fromage)* and dessert. Dessert and cheese are frequently offered as alternatives. Tap water *(eau en carafe)* and bread *(pain)* are automatically provided with your meal. A *café* or *déca* (decaffeinated coffee) should not be forgotten.

An extensive wine list is the sign of a good restaurant. Wine *(vin)* is only served during a meal, never after. A tip *(pourboire)* of 5–10 percent is de rigueur.

BRASSERIES

Brasseries are very much part of the Paris scene. As opposed to a small, cosy bistro with a modest menu, brasseries are fairly large restaurants which sprang up at the turn of the 20th century and served hearty fare in addition to seafood specialities. Many brasseries hold the distinction as a protected historical site with their glamorous Belle-Époque décor. Though the food is not exactly cheap in these restaurants, it is still relatively affordable *(Moderate)*.

BOFINGER ● (148 B6) *(𝄞 O9)*
The *choucroute de la mer,* sauerkraut with fish and other seafood, is a hit, served in a striking Art Nouveau setting under a glass dome. *Daily | 5–7, rue*

01 43 20 14 20 | M 4 Vavin | www.lacoupole-paris.com

JULIEN ★ (147 F2) *(𝄞 M6)*
Extravagant stucco decorations between vine-covered Art Nouveau maidens plus colourful glass ceilings with mirrored walls will fascinate all those

Bohemians met at Les Deux Magots back in the 1920s

Bastille | 4th arr. | tel. 01 42 72 87 82 | M 1, 5, 8 Bastille | www.bofingerparis.com

BRASSERIE LIPP (146 B6) *(𝄞 K8)*
Famous restaurant founded in 1880 by an Alsatian. Frequented by statesmen and literati. *Daily | 151, bd. Saint-Germain | 6th arr. | tel. 01 45 48 53 91 | M 4 Saint-Germain-des-Prés*

LA COUPOLE ★ (152 B3) *(𝄞 J10)*
In the 1920s, artists such as Chagall, Picasso and Dalí kept company in this Art Deco temple. The 33 columns in this largest brasserie in Paris, which operates as a café during the day, have been designed by artists. *Daily | 120, bd. du Montparnasse | 14th arr. | tel.*

who dine in this long-standing brasserie. *Daily | 16, rue du Faubourg Saint-Denis | 10th arr. | tel. 01 47 70 12 06 | M 4, 8, 9 Strasbourg-Saint-Denis | www.julienparis.com*

CAFÉS

INSIDER TIP ► ANGÉLINA
(146 B3) *(𝄞 J7)*
Classics from one of the most sophisticated cafés in the city are the hot chocolate and the "Montblanc", a sumptuous half scoop of meringue and chestnut purée. *Daily | 226, rue de Rivoli | 1st arr. | tel. 01 42 60 82 00 | M 1 Tuileries | www.angelina-paris.fr*

CAFÉ DE FLORE (146 B6) (*Ⅲ K8*)
An institution and meeting place for artists, literary figures and intellectuals since Simone de Beauvoir, Jean-Paul Sartre and Albert Camus were regulars here. Today, it is a place to see and be seen among the best and brightest. *Daily | 172, bd. Saint-Germain | 6th arr. | tel. 0145485526 | M 4 Saint-Germain-des-Prés | www.cafedeflore.fr*

LADURÉE (146 A3) (*Ⅲ J6*)
Ostentatious *salon de thé* from the 19th century with richly painted ceiling frescoes. Especially famed for its marvellous macarons, offered in every conceivable colour and flavour, which can also be taken home like many of the other delectable creations. *Daily | 16, rue Royale | 8th arr. | tel. 0142602179 | M 8, 12, 14 Madeleine | www.laduree.fr*

LES DEUX MAGOTS (146 B6) (*Ⅲ K8*)
This famous "café littéraire" – according to its justifiable self-promotion – where Ernest Hemingway came to drink whiskey is named after the two Chinese porcelain figures at the entrance. It is a special treat to sit on the terrace facing Saint-Germain-des-Prés. *Daily | 6, pl. Saint-Germain-des-Prés | 6th arr. | tel. 0145485525 | M 4 Saint-Germain-des-Prés | www.lesdeuxmagots.fr*

MARIAGE FRÈRES (138 C6) (*Ⅲ F5*)
Tea salon decorated in the elegant Colonial style with an unbeatable array of teas. Accessories and exquisite baked goods complement the experience. The lunch menu features dishes refined with tea. **INSIDER TIP** *Tea museum* on the first floor. *Daily | 30–32, rue du Bourg-Tibourg | 8th arr. | tel. 0142 72 26 11 | M 1, 11 Hôtel de Ville | www.mariagefreres.fr*

LA PALETTE (146 C6) (*Ⅲ K8*)
A terrace café close to the art academy that is lively both at lunchtime and in the evening. A fin-de-siècle masterpiece. *Daily | 43, rue de Seine | 6th arr. | tel. 0143 26 68 15 | M 4 Saint-Germain-des-Prés | www.cafelapaletteparis.com*

RESTAURANTS: EXPENSIVE

BEL CANTO ★ (147 E5) (*Ⅲ M8*)
A unique restaurant in which trained opera singers, accompanied by a piano, belt out arias by Verdi, Puccini and others as you enjoy the fine Italian cuisine. A dining experience based on the motto "les

---

★ **La Coupole**
Art Déco temple for artists → p. 62

★ **Julien**
Paris' most splendidly decorated brasserie → p. 62

★ **Bel Canto**
The finest Italian cuisine accompanied by arias → p. 63

★ **Le Bélier**
Small but noble gem → p. 64

★ **Les Ombres**
Contemporary restaurant with a view of the Eiffel Tower → p. 65

★ **Le Train Bleu**
Majestic fin-de-siècle decor – a feast for the senses → p. 65

★ **L'Escargot Montorgueil**
Upscale traditional restaurant from the time of Les Halles → p. 66

MARCO POLO HIGHLIGHTS

diners lyriques". *Daily (evenings only) | 72, quai de l'Hôtel de Ville | 4th arr. | tel. 01 42 78 30 18 | M 1, 11 Hôtel de Ville | www.lebelcanto.com*

LE BÉLIER ★
(146 C5) (*Ø K8*)

This illustrious restaurant evokes the paintings of the Dutch painter Jan Vermeer. Star designer Jacques Garcia has transformed this intimate restaurant in the elegant *L'Hôtel* into a real gem. The comfortable armchairs and unobtrusive classical music in the background make it easy to understand why writer and aesthete Oscar Wilde spent the last days of his life here. Considering the atmosphere and history, lunches are quite affordable. *Daily (Aug closed Sun/Mon) | 13, rue des Beaux Arts | 6th arr. |*

GOURMET RESTAURANTS

Alain Ducasse au Plaza Athénée
(145 D3) (*Ø G6*)

The restaurant of the identically named hotel welcomes its guests with original designs of different styles. The chef Alain Ducasse is one of the culinary greats. Set menu from 360 euros. *Closed Sat/Sun (Mon–Wed for dinner only) | 25, av. Montaigne | 8th arr. | tel. 01 53 67 65 00 | M 1, 9 Franklin D. Roosevelt | www.alain-ducasse.com*

L'Abeille (144 B3) (*Ø F7*)

Dine like Napoleon, or more accurately said like his nephew Prince Roland Bonaparte who once resided here. Michelin star chef Phillippe Labbé bewitches with his *menu dégustation* (225 euros) of delicacies such as spring lamb, blue lobster or foie gras in chocolate. *Closed Sun/Mon | Hotel Shangri-La | 10, av. d'Iena | 16th arr. | tel. 01 53 67 19 90 | M 9 Iéna | www.shangri-la.com*

Le Grand Véfour (146 C3) (*Ø K6*)

The lavishly gilded décor in the Palais Royal is the perfect environment for first-class cuisine. Set menu from 268 euros. *Closed Sat/Sun (open on Fri only for lunch) | 17, rue Beaujolais | 1st arr. | tel. 01 42 96 56 27 | M 1, 7 Palais Royal-Musée du Louvre | www.grand-vefour.com*

Jules Verne ✷ (144 B5) (*Ø F8*)

Where you can savour Alain Ducasse's exclusive cuisine and have Paris at your feet. Set menu from 185 euros. *Daily | lift to the 2nd floor of the Eiffel Tower | 7th arr. | tel. 01 45 55 61 44 | M 6 Bir Hakeim | www.lejulesverne-paris.com*

Le Meurice (146 B3) (*Ø J7*)

The dining room in this restaurant run by Alain Ducasse is absolutely beautiful. Set menu from 380 euros. *Closed Sat/Sun | 228, rue de Rivoli | 1st arr. | tel. 01 44 58 10 55 | M 1 Tuileries | www.lemeurice.com*

Pierre Gagnaire (145 D2) (*Ø F5*)

The restaurant decor where the three-star-chef Pierre Gagnaire holds court is not all that's modern, his culinary creations are also incredibly innovative. Set menu from 235 euros. *Closed Sat (Sun dinner only, in Aug lunch only) | Hotel Balzac | 6, rue Balzac | 8th arr. | tel. 01 58 36 12 50 | M 1 George V | www.pierre-gagnaire.com*

tel. 01 44 41 99 00 | M 4 Saint-Germain-des-Prés | www.l-hotel.com

CITRUS ETOILE (144 C1) (*M F5*)

Excellent cuisine – classical French dishes with a modern interpretation including Asian and Californian influences – originate from Gilles Epié's kitchen. Comfortably discreet atmosphere and only a few yards from the Arc de Triomphe. Daily (*Sat/Sun for private functions only) | 6, rue Arséne Houssaye | 8th arr. | tel. 01 42 89 15 51 | M 1, 2, 6 Etoile | RER A Etoile | www.citrusetoile.fr*

HIRAMATSU (144 A3) (*M E7*)

Critics are excited about this "Japanese Alain Ducasse". Hiroyuki Hiramatsu, the cuisiniere-en-chef from the Far East, conjures up classic French dishes in his unique way for restaurant guests. Absolutely delicious! Closed *Sat/Sun | 52, rue de Longchamp | 16th arr. | tel. 01 56 81 08 80 | M 6, 9 Trocadéro | www. hiramatsu.co.jp/fr*

LES OMBRES ★ ⚘
(136 C4) (*M F7*)

You will not find a more spectacular view of the Eiffel Tower than through the glass roof of this restaurant at the Musée du Quai Branly. In the summer you can enjoy the meals imaginatively prepared by Jean-François Oyon and the exquisite atmosphere from the terrace. *Daily | 27, quai Branly | 7th arr. | tel. 01 47 53 68 00 | M 9 Iéna | www.lesombres-restaurant. com*

1728 (146 A2) (*M J6*)

An upscale restaurant in four seemingly private salons lavishly decorated with antiques. Time seems to have stood still in these rooms where Madame Pompadour was once a regular guest. Thanks to the owner, a Chinesian musician, the

Champagne served in style at the Le Grand Véfour

ambiance and the food have acquired a slight Asian touch over the course of extensive renovations. *Mon/Sat lunch only, closed Sunday | 8, rue d'Anjou | 8th arr. | tel. 01 40 17 04 77 | M 1, 8, 12 Concorde | www.restaurant-1728.com*

LE TRAIN BLEU ★ ●
(154 C2) (*M O–P10*)

Without a doubt the most exquisite station restaurant in the world. The 20-foot-high ceilings are reminiscent of a dining hall at Versailles. Should you find the prices for the classic French cuisine too prohibitive, opt for a cocktail and enjoy the glorious atmosphere in one of the comfortable leather armchairs in the bar.

Daily | pl. Louis Armand | 12th arr. | tel. 01 43 43 09 06 | M 1, 14 Gare de Lyon | RER A, D Gare de Lyon | www.le-train-bleu.com

RESTAURANTS: MODERATE

ALCAZAR (146 C6) *(ᗰ K8)*

The meeting place for the jet set crowd bears Sir Terence Conran's trademark. The bar on the upper floor boasts the best DJs in the city. The cuisine pulls out all the stops when it comes to classic French dishes according to the motto "back to tradition". *Daily | 62, rue Mazarine | 6th arr. | tel. 01 53 10 19 99 | M 4, 10 Odéon | www.alcazar.fr*

Au Vieux Paris: blossoming purple wisteria adorns the entrance and courtyard

BOUILLON RACINE (153 D1) *(ᗰ L9)*

Gorgeous Art Nouveau ornamentation winds around two storeys of windows, mirrors and wood panelling in a pleasing shade of green. Even the mosaic floor has been meticulously restored in this former workers' cafeteria. The cuisine with a Belgian touch is equally meticulously prepared. *Daily | 3, rue Racine | 6th arr. | tel. 01 44 32 15 60 | M 10 Cluny-La Sorbonne | RER B Cluny-La Sorbonne | www.bouillon-racine.com*

CAFÉ MARLY ● ⬩
(146 C4) *(ᗰ K7)*

Chic restaurant with a INSIDER TIP stellar view of the Louvre from the terrace. Modern French cuisine and tasty noodle dishes. The establishment draws a young, international crowd, especially during the Parisian fashion weeks. *Daily | Palais du Louvre | 93, rue de Rivoli | 1st arr. | tel. 01 49 26 06 60 | M 1, 7 Palais Royal-Musée du Louvre | www.cafe-marly.com*

CHANTAIRELLE (153 E2) *(ᗰ M10)*

This restaurant pays homage to the Auvergne. With the exception of the ice cream, everything on the menu originates from this region in central France. The hearty and succulent cuisine suits the rustic atmosphere and the small but attractive courtyard. You can even take items home from their deli, including cold meat, cheese and lentils. *Daily (lunch only on Sun/Mon, dinner only on Sat and in Aug) | 17, rue Laplace | 5th arr. | tel. 01 46 33 18 59 | M 10 Cardinal Lemoine | www.chantairelle.com*

L'ESCARGOT MONTORGUEIL ★
(147 E4) *(ᗰ L7)*

A traditional restaurant established in 1832, decorated in the Empire style. Luminaries such as Marcel Proust, Charlie

Chaplin, Pablo Picasso and Jacqueline Kennedy have dined here. The entrance is decorated with a ceiling painting from the dining room of the famous actress Sarah Bernhardt. The eponymous escargot, as well as first-class dishes from the former market hall that once stood next door, feature on the menu. *Daily | 38, rue Montorgueil | 1st arr. | tel. 01 42 36 83 51 | M 4 Etienne Marcel | www. escargotmontorgueil.com*

INSIDER TIP ▶ **AU VIEUX PARIS** (147 E6) (*M8*)
Located next to Notre-Dame, this is where the canons lived back in 1512. Today, the owners Odette and Georges de Larochebrochard cordially welcome their guests. Traditional French cuisine has been served here since 1750! The exuberantly plush furnishings with a Gothic touch create a romantic atmosphere; the set meal is substantial and not expensive by Parisian standards. *Closed Sat lunch | 24, rue Chanoinesse | 4th arr. | tel. 01 40 51 78 52 | M 4 Cité | www.auvieuxparis.fr*

LA GARE (156 B4) (*C8*)
Tables in this converted railway station have been cleverly placed under a skylight between the tracks that can still be seen. Light, international cuisine, good lunch menu (Mon–Fri). The bar and terrace in this chic district of Passy are à la mode. Occasional theme nights, Sun brunch until 3pm (35 euros), DJs at weekends. *Daily | 19, ch. de la Muette | 16th arr. | tel. 01 42 15 15 31 | M 9 La Muette | www.restaurantlagare.com*

MACEO (146 C3) (*L6*)
Innovative, contemporary restaurant with a large, light and comfortable dining area. Also serves vegetarian dishes. A small library and bar entice you to linger a little longer. *Closed Sat for lunch and Sun | 15, rue des Petits-Champs | 1st arr. | tel. 01 42 97 53 85 | M 3 Bourse | www.maceorestaurant.com*

LE P'TIT TROQUET (145 D5) (*G8*)
Tiny bistro with an authentic 1920s flair serving sophisticated and refined traditional French cuisine such as "homemade foie gras with fig chutney". A good value for the money, especially considering its close proximity to the Eiffel Tower. *Closed Mon/Sat lunch and Sundays | 28, rue de l'Exposition | 7th arr. | tel. 01 47 05 80 39 | M8 Ecole Militaire*

INSIDER TIP ▶ **RIAD NEJMA** (147 E4) (*M7*)
In this spacious restaurant directly across from the Centre Pompidou, the ambiance is reminiscent of the tales of *One Thousand and One Nights*. Enjoy excellent Moroccan dishes complimented with belly dancers and eaten under palm trees. *Daily (Mon–Thu evenings only) | 141, rue Saint-Martin | 3rd arr. | tel. 01 42 78 35 00 | M 11 Rambuteau | www. riadnejma.com*

INSIDER TIP ▶ **LE SUD** (138 A6) (*E4*)
Guests have the feeling of being in a village in the South of France under a vaulted glass roof. Pleasant atmosphere, friendly service and tasty Provençal specialities. A reservation is necessary at this much-loved restaurant. *Daily | 91, bd. Gouvion Saint Cyr | 17th arr. | tel. 01 45 74 02 77 | M 1 Porte Maillot | RER C Porte Maillot | www.le-sud-restaurant. com*

RESTAURANTS: BUDGET

BISTROT RICHELIEU (146 C3) (*K7*)
The comfortable atmosphere in this restaurant is exactly what you need after an exhausting visit to the neighbour-

ing Louvre. Typical French dishes such as snails, onion soup and duck grace the tables. *Closed Sat lunch/Sundays | 45, rue de Richelieu | 1st arr. | tel. 01 42 60 19 16 | M 1 Palais Royal | www.bistrotrichelieu.fr*

INSIDER TIP CALIFE (146 C5) (*∅ K8*)
The ideal place for romantic couples to eat: this two-hour cruise (9pm–11pm) past the islands in the Seine comes with a three-course menu for 67 euros. The boat has been lovingly restored by its owner, a musician – and there are occasional music performances. Make

reservations well in advance! *Daily | quai Malaquais | near Pont des Arts | 6th arr. | tel. 01 43 54 50 04 | M 1 Louvre-Rivoli | www.calife.com*

CHEZ MARIANNE (147 F5) (*∅ N8*)
This busy restaurant with a terrace and a delicatessen is located around the corner from the lively rue des Rosiers at the centre of the Marais district. Try the popular Middle Eastern appetiser platter. Reservations are a must. *Daily | 2, rue des Hospitalières Saint-Gervais | 4th arr. | tel. 01 42 72 18 86 | M 1 Saint-Paul*

CHOUCHOU (147 E4) (*∅ M7*)
A restaurant offering affordable North African and French meals with live piano music on its terrace. The meals are served by friendly waiters. *Daily | 63, rue Rambuteau | 3rd arr. | tel. 01 42 77 37 30 | M 4 Les Halles*

HOPE CAFÉ ◉
(141 D3) (*∅ L3*)
Located behind Sacré-Cœur, this modern restaurant with its own food shop specializes in organic foods. It goes without saying that there are plenty of vegetarian options. The smoothies are particularly popular. *Closed Sun/Mon | 64, rue Lamarck | 18th arr. | tel. 01 46 06 54 40 | M 12 Lamarck-Caulaincourt | www.hope -cafe.com*

INSIDER TIP LA FOURMI AILÉE
(153 E1) (*∅ M9*)
"The winged ant" is a very trendy place. As a former library, this restaurant and café only a few steps from Notre-Dame has a cosy and casual atmosphere. The large selection of teas and the many snacks make it perfect for a little break. *Daily | 8, rue du Fouarre | 5th arr. | tel. 01 43 29 40 99 | | M 10 Cluny-La Sorbonne | www.parisresto.com*

LOW BUDGET

The African district is home to *Le Tribal Café* ● (147 E1) (*∅ M5*) *(daily | 3, cour des Petites Ecuries | 10th arr. | tel. 01 47 70 57 08 | M 4 Château-d'Eau)* where you can dine for free – though a small contribution of 3.50 euros for drinks is expected – in an exotic and convivial atmosphere: Fri/Sat *couscous*, Wed/Thu *moules frites* (mussels with chips), from 9pm.

Vegetarian fare is available at the Indian restaurant *Krishna Bhavan* (142 A5) (*∅ N4*) *(daily | 24, rue Cail | 10th arr. | tel. 01 42 05 78 43 | M 2 La Chapelle)* – delicious currys from 4.50 euros and soups for 3 euros.

Inexpensive specialities from southwest France and the Basque region at the modest restaurant *Chez Gladines* (153 E6) (*∅ M12*) *(daily | 30, rue des Cinq Diamants | 13th arr. | tel. 01 45 80 70 10 | M 6 Corvisart | www. gladines-restaurant-paris.fr)* in the nightlife district Butte-aux-Cailles.

LA FRESQUE
(147 E4) (∅ M7)

Located directly adjacent to the shopping centre Les Halles, this small restaurant not only has good-natured waiters, but also a typically Parisian flair. Good value for money. It is always full in the

Mon | 30, rue Gay Lussac | 5th arr. | tel. 01 43 25 20 79 | RER B Luxembourg | www.lespapillesparis.fr

PAUSE CAFÉ 148 C6) (∅ P9)

In the afternoon, it's a typical café with a sunny terrace. Otherwise, it's a colourful

Peruse – discuss – sample: the selection is impossibly irresistible at Chez Marianne

evenings. *Closed Sun | 100, rue Rambuteau | 1st arr. | tel. 01 42 33 17 56 | M 4 Les Halles | www.restaurant-la-fesque-paris.fr*

LE MESTURET
(146 C2) (∅ L6)

Fresh bistro fare served by friendly staff – it's no wonder it was once voted the best bistro of the year. *Daily | 77, rue de Richelieu | 2nd arr. | tel. 01 42 97 40 68 | M 3 Bourse | www.lemesturet.com*

LES PAPILLES
(153 D3) (∅ L10)

Bistro with a wine cellar and delicatessen. Serves authentic cuisine near the Jardin du Luxembourg. *Closed Sun/*

trendy spot with Italianate food located directly behind the Bastille. A perennial favourite whose popularity has not waned over the years. *Daily (Sun only until 8pm) | 41, rue de Charonne | 11th arr. | tel. 01 40 21 89 06 | M 1, 5, 8 Bastille*

À LA POMPONNETTE
(140 C4) (∅ K3)

Time seems to have stood still here at the foot of Montmartre. This bar and restaurant serves generous helpings of hearty, traditional French food. *Daily | 42, rue Lepic | 18th arr. | tel. 01 46 06 08 36 | M 2 Place Blanche | www.pomponnette-montmartre.com*

LOCAL SPECIALITIES

bœuf bourguignon – braised beef in a Burgundy sauce

bouillabaisse – fish stew made with Mediterranean fish

brochettes de coquilles Saint Jacques – kebabs with scallops

caneton à l'orange – roast duck in an orange sauce (photo right)

coq au vin – braise of chicken in red wine, but sometimes in Riesling

côtes de porc aux herbes – pork chops with herbs

crème brûlée – a rich custard base topped with a layer of hard caramel

crêpes Suzette – thin pancakes with Grand Marnier

écrevisses à la nage – boiled crayfish in a spicy broth

escargots à la bourguignonne – boiled Burgundy snails served in their shells

fruits de mer – seafood, e.g. *crevettes* (prawns, photo left) or *huîtres* (oysters) – often served raw

gigot d'agneau aux morilles – leg of lamb with morels

gratin dauphinois – potato gratin

homard à l'armoricaine – lobster in a tomato, garlic, herb, white wine and cognac sauce

moules marinières – mussels steamed in white wine with onions

noisettes d'agneau – small lamb cutlets fried in butter

pot-au-feu – stew with beef, chicken and a variety of vegetables

profiteroles – small cream puff-pastry with vanilla ice cream and chocolate sauce

quenelles de brochet – pickerel, cream and egg dumplings

ratatouille – vegetables sauteed with olive oil, onions and herbs, served either hot or cold

soupe à l'oignon gratinée – onion soup baked with cheese

tarte Tatin – carmelised upside down apple tart

SATURNE

(147 D2) (*Ø L6*)

Trendy restaurant with austere wooden furnishings under a glass roof and an excellent vinotheque in the lobby. The fresh, uncomplicated cuisine is outstanding. *Closed Sat/Sun | 17, rue Notre-Dame-des-Victoires | 2nd arr. | tel. 01 42 60 31 90 | M 3 Bourse | www.saturne-paris.fr*

WINEBARS

The wine list in a *bar à vins* vins is of course extensive and snacks such as meat and cheese plates are often served.

INSIDER TIP LE BARON ROUGE
(154 C1) (*ω P9*)

A small wine bar with a special flair. It is particularly lively in the Baron Rouge, on Sundays when, after shopping at the nearby *Marché d'Aligre*, the Parisians stand together around wine barrels in front of the bar enjoying a glass of wine and oysters. *Daily | 1, rue Théophile-Roussel | 12th arr. | tel. 01 43 43 14 32 | M 8 Ledru-Rollin*

LE COUDE FOU
(147 F5) (*ω N8*)

A typical wine bar, sadly rare in Paris. Large selection, simple wooden tables and snacks upon request. *Daily |* 12, rue du Bourg-Tibourg | 4th arr. | tel. 01 42 77 15 16 | M 1, 11 Hôtel de Ville | www.lecoudefou.com

JUVÈNILES
(146 C4) (*ω K6*)

This bar is very popular, especially among the younger crowd, and not only because of the tasty appetisers and tapas. *Closed Sun/Mon lunchtime | 47, rue de Richelieu | 1st arr. | tel. 01 42 97 46 49 | M 1, 7 Palais Royal-Musée du Louvre*

LE RUBIS
(146 B3) (*ω K6*)

A simple wine bar that has remained virtually unchanged since its opening in 1948. Large wine selection, cheese platter and a traditional daily special. *Closed Sat dinner/Sundays | 10, rue du Marché Saint-Honoré | 1st arr. | tel. 01 42 61 03 34 | M 8, 14 Pyramides*

Le Rubis: chatting over a glass of red wine with friends and neighbours

SHOPPING

🏙 WHERE TO START?

If you're not looking for cheap clothing or practically unwearable haute couture and want to avoid the stress of department store clutter, you're best off in **Marais (148 A–B 3–6) (🗺 M–O 6–8)**. You'll find plenty of shops where French women buy their working day wardrobe. Men can also find what they're looking for in shops here too. Select hand-crafted items and cosmetics round off your shopping spree and a break at one of the street cafés in the district always turns shopping into a pleasurable event.

Shopping in the French consumer metropolis conjures up images of fashion, perfumes, delicatessens, champagne and other luxury items. In Paris, everything is done to the hilt and products are always showcased with élan.

A shopping spree in Paris means digging deeper into your pockets than at home. Paris offers the best of everything and, if you know where to shop, you can even land a good bargain. Apart from that, wandering through the shrines to consumerism and shopping streets, *lèche vitrines* (window shopping), as they say in French, has sheer entertainment value. Whether it's the haute couture shop windows or a grocery store's lavish and colourful displays: shopping in Paris is an

Très chic, très riche: high-quality fashion, accessories and delicatessens with enticing displays are *de rigueur*

experience. Some even make a special trip to take advantage of clearance sales *(soldes)* that occur twice a year (Jan and June/July).

Most shops are open Monday–Saturday from 10am to 7:30pm. On Thursdays large department stores have longer opening hours known as *nocturne,* evening shopping, and close at either 9pm or 10pm. If you want to shop on Sunday, stores in Marais, the lower ground floor at the Louvre and some shops on the Champs-Elysées are open. Many of the small grocers *(épiceries)* never seem to close: in France there is no law regulating closing time for shops. Note, however, that some of the smaller stores close on Monday, Wednesday, or over lunchtime. Department stores and many other shops are open on the last three or four Sundays before Christmas. Opening hours are only listed in this section if they differ from the norm.

First-class caviar is only one of the specialities to be found at Fauchon

ANTIQUES

DROUOT (146 C1) (*Ø L5*)

As one of the oldest auction houses in the world, Drouot is an institution. Furniture and art objects come under the hammer in 21 halls. Like a visit to a museum! *9, rue Drouot | 9th arr. | M 8, 9 Richelieu-Drouot | www.drouot.com*

INSIDER TIP VILLAGE SAINT-PAUL
(148 A6) (*Ø N8*)

90 different shops are situated in several interconnected, idyllic back courtyards near the Place des Vosges where you'll find small pieces of furniture, paintings, jewellery, porcelain and more. *Thu–Mon | between rue Saint-Paul and rue Charlemagne | 4th arr. | M 1 Saint-Paul*

BOOKS & MUSIC

LES BOUQUINISTES
(146–147 B–E 4–6) (*Ø K–M 7–8*)

The green wooden boxes on both sides of the Seine have shaped the cityscape for more than 300 years. It's a real kick to rummage through the old books, newspapers and postcards. *Between Jardin des Tuileries and the Île Saint-Louis | 1st arr./5th arr. | M 7 Pont Neuf*

FNAC ●
(145 D2) (*Ø G6*)

The largest bookseller in Paris also has a large CD and DVD department. An excellent place to while away a few hours on a rainy day. *Daily until 11:45pm | 74, av. des Champs-Elysées | 8th arr. | M 1, 9 Franklin D. Roosevelt | www.fnac.com*

VIRGIN MEGASTORE
(145 D2) (*Ø G6*)

Huge CD store where you could easily spend hours browsing. (CDs are more expensive here than at home!) *Daily until midnight | 52, av. des Champs-Elysées | 8th arr. | M 1, 9: Franklin D. Roosevelt | www.virgin megastore.fr*

DELICATESSEN

AMORINO (153 F1) *(🕮 M9)*
In 2002, two Italians opened the first artisan ice cream boutique on the Île Saint-Louis, and there are now 19 stores in Paris. *Daily noon –midnight (closed Dec–Feb) | 47, rue Saint-Louis-en-Île | 4th arr. | M 7 Pont Marie*

BARTHÉLEMY ⭐ (146 A6) *(🕮 J8)*
One of the best cheese emporiums *(crèmeries)* in Paris, it also caters to Élysée Palace. Former President Charles de Gaulle once remarked: "How can anyone govern a nation that has two hundred and forty-six different kinds of cheese?" The aromas of many of these cheeses waft through this small shop. *51, rue de Grenelle | 7th arr. | M 12 Rue du Bac*

DEBAUVE & GALLAIS ⭐
(146 B5) *(🕮 K8)*
The opulent, 200-year-old chocolaterie can be compared to a jewellery shop. The big difference: these gems melt in your mouth. *30, rue des Saint-Pères | 7th arr. | M 4 Saint-Germain-des-Prés | www.debauve-et-gallais.com*

FAUCHON (146 A2) *(🕮 J6)*
Gourmands and ordinary consumers alike can appreciate the celestial selection of exotic fruits, truffles and caviar in this gourmet shop. *26, pl. de la Madeleine | 8th arr. | M 8, 12, 14 Madeleine | www.fauchon.fr*

HÉDIARD (146 A2) *(🕮 J6)*
This long standing delicatessen (founded in 1854) is known for its variety of treats in exquisitely packed little tins, especially the truffled foie gras and lobster pâté, which make appropriate souvenirs. *21, pl. de la Madeleine | 8th arr. | M 8, 12, 14 Madeleine | www.hediard.fr*

INSIDER TIP IZRAËL (147 F5) *(🕮 N8)*
Specialities from all over the world, mainly Arabian, African and Asian countries, are piled to the rafters in wild confusion amid the sausages hanging from hooks and the exotic spices. A unique aromatic experience. *30, rue François Miron | 4th arr. | M 1 Saint-Paul*

LAVINIA (146 B2) *(🕮 J6)*
The largest wine cellar in Europe. 7,500 wines from 43 countries on three storeys in a price range from 3 to 6,500 euros. You can test the wine (without a surcharge) together with a snack in the accompanying bar. *3–5, bd. de la Madeleine | 1st arr. | M 8, 12, 14 Madeleine | www.lavinia.fr*

MARCO POLO HIGHLIGHTS

⭐ **Barthélemy**
A paradise for cheese lovers within a tiny space → p. 75

⭐ **Debauve & Gallais**
A chocolaterie which resembles an upscale jewellery store → p. 75

⭐ **Marché aux Puces**
Probably the world's largest flea market, in Saint-Ouen → p. 77

⭐ **Le Bon Marché**
The most elegant department store in all of Paris → p. 78

⭐ **Rue du Faubourg Saint-Honoré**
The haute couture area of the city → p. 78

⭐ **Place des Victoires**
Young fashion designers and lots of boutiques → p. 79

LEGRAND FILLES & FILS
(146 C3) (*ω L6*)

A mouth-watering delicatessen shop situated between the nostalgic Galleries Vivienne and rue de la Banque. The shop was established in 1880 and exudes time-honoured elegance. Wine connoisseurs in particular will clamour to experience the extensive wine selection and wine tastings at the bar's wooden counters. *1, rue de la Banque | 2nd arr. | M 1 Palais-Royal | www.caves-legrand.com*

INSIDER TIP ▶ MAISON STOHRER
(147 D3) (*ω L6*)

What a dream! This shop is like a blast from the past. The oldest confectionary in Paris was established in 1730. The court pastry chef who founded it came to Paris from Poland along with Maria Leszczyńska when she married Louis XV. Even today, delicacies such as the *baba au rhum* are made according to the old recipes. *51, rue Montorgueil | 2nd arr. | www.stohrer.fr | M 3 Sentier*

MAISON DE THÉ GEORGE CANNON ●
● (152 B2) (*ω J10*)

A great selection of teas awaits you here: you can choose from over 250 types of tea. The venerable establishment is much more than a tea shop. In addition to tastings in the bar, light organic dishes are served in the salon. Shiatsu massages or an authentic Japanese tea ceremony on the shop's lower level are a good way to unwind. *Tue–Sat 10:30am–7:30pm | 12, Notre-Dame-des Champs | 6th arr. | M 4 St.-Placide | www.georgecannon.fr*

LA PÂTISSERIE DES RÊVES
(146 A6) (*ω J9*)

Tartes au citron, mille-feuilles, éclaires ... decadent indulgences of French confectionary art await under bell jars and entice you to buy and savour. Tue–Sat

9am–8pm, Sun 9am–4pm | 93, rue du Bac | 7th arr. | M 12 Rue du Bac | www. lapatisseriedesreves.com

INSIDER TIP ▶ ROSE BAKERY ●
(148 C6) (*ω L4*)

The absolute "in" place among young and dynamic Parisian "bobos" who love to enjoy English-style baked goods or the imaginative vegetarian snacks made with organic ingredients in minimalist surroundings. *46, rue des Martyrs | 9th arr. | M 12 Saint-Georges*

DESIGN & LIFESTYLE

ARTY DANDY
146 B6) (*ω K8*)

A shop for those who have everything. It sees itself as a gallery-store, and anything in terms of art, kitsch, fashion, cosmetics and design as well as the extraordinary, including individual pieces and limited editions, can be bought here. *1, rue de Furstemberg | 6th arr. | M 4 St.-Germain-des-Prés | www.arty dandy.com*

DEHILLERIN
(147 D4) (*ω L7*)

In this shop, steeped in tradition since 1820, you will find everything that has to do with kitchens and cooking on its two floors. Dehillerin is world-renowned among chefs and French celebrity chefs also frequent this shop. *18, rue Coquillière | 1st arr. | M/RER Châtelet-Les Halles | www.e-dehillerin.fr*

MARCHÉ SAINT PIERRE
(149 D4) (*ω L3*)

Covering five floors and over 26,900 square feet, this somewhat older department store stocks rolls of fabric at unbeatable prices. Many women from the nearby African neighbourhood scour the shelves for the right materials. Rows of fabric shops line the whole area in this paradise for those who sew. *2, rue Charles Nodier | 18th arr. | M2 Anvers*

NATURE ET DÉCOUVERTES
(146 C4) (*⌀ K7*)

Stocked with everything related to personal well-being from relaxing CDs, scents and teas to garden accessories and unusual toys, this shop is a place of tranquility amidst the buzzing shopping centre Forum des Halles. *10 bis, rue de l'Arc en Ciel | 1st arr. | M 4 Les Halles | www.natureetdecouvertes.com*

FLEA MARKETS

ALIGRE
(154 C1) (*⌀ P9*)

The very beautiful Marché d'Aligre is the oldest flea market in Paris. The prices are quite affordable and even groceries can be purchased here. *Tue–Sun mornings | 1e, pl. d'Aligre | 12th arr. | M 8 Ledru-Rollin*

SAINT-OUEN ★
(140–141 C–E1) (*⌀ K–L1*)

With more than 3,000 stalls, the *Marché aux Puces de Saint-Ouen* is the world's largest flea market. You can purchase almost everything here. The grounds at the Porte de Clignancourt encompass a range of various markets. To see them all you'll have to cover around 10 miles. For a bit of refreshment along the way, we recommend the rustic tavern *Chez Louisette (130, av. Michelet)* with live music on the *Marché Vernaison (www.vernaison.net)*. *Sat 9am–6pm, Sun 10am–6pm, Mon 11am–5pm | 18th arr. | M 4 Porte de Clignancourt*

VANVES (151 D6) (*⌀ O*)

The Marché aux Puces de la Porte de Vanves, covering no more than two

The whole *marché aux puces* in Saint-Ouen is as colourful as these pictures

streets, is the smallest flea market in Paris. On one street, you'll find a mix of new and old clothes, shoes and handbags, while the other one is a haven for novelties and furniture of all kinds. *Sat/ Sun 7am–6pm | av. Georges Lafenestre | 14th arr. | M 13 Porte de Vanves | www. pucesdevanves.typepad.com*

DEPARTMENT STORES

LE BON MARCHÉ ★ (152 A1) (*J9*)

The oldest department store in Paris and a symbol of luxury and quality for over 150 years. It is still a joy to meander through this Belle-Époque gem with

Trendy shoes by Monderer can be found on rue des Francs-Bourgeois

unobtrusive classical music in the background, away from the usual touristy hustle and bustle. One of the best shoe and fashion departments carrying all the big-name brands. The gourmet food section next to it is quite an experience! *24, rue de Sèvres | 7th arr. | M 10, 12 Sèvres Babylone | www.lebonmarche.fr | www. lagrandeepicerie.fr*

GALERIES LAFAYETTE (146 B1) (*K5*)

The shrine to consumerism situated under a massive glass dome has been a huge attraction since 1908. Clothing is arranged by brand name, as opposed to the type of garment (trousers, shirts, etc.) The shoe department is the largest in the world covering nearly 10,000 square feet. If you need a break from shopping, a variety of restaurants offer something to suit every taste. *40, bd. Haussmann | 9th arr. | M 3, 7, 8 Opéra | RER A Auber | www.gale rieslafayette.com*

LE PRINTEMPS (146 C1) (*K5*)

In addition to the huge cosmetics department on the ground floor and the beautiful spa area on the first floor, the upper floor is devoted to all the luxury fashion brands as well as less costly labels beyond the café-restaurant under the famous Art Nouveau glass dome. *64, bd. Haussmann | 9th arr. | M 3, 9 Havre-Caumartin | RER A Auber | www.printemps.com*

WHAT TO WEAR & ACCESSORIES

On *Avenue Montaigne* (145 D3)(*G6*) and ★ ● *rue du Faubourg Saint-Honoré* (146 A–B3)(*H–K 5–6)*, the "Triangle d'Or" of luxury boutiques, you'll find all the well-known names in fashion: Armani, Chanel, Dior, Gucci, Hermès, Lacroix, Max Mara, Versace, etc.

Younger and bolder fashion labels are located around the ⭐ *Place des Victoires* (147 D3) (*📖 L6*) while designers such as Kenzo, Gaultier and others are sold in boutiques on r*ue Etienne Marcel.* In Marais, especially in and around *rue des Francs-Bourgeois* (148 A–B5) (*📖 N–O8*) more unconventional fashion boutiques such as Abu d'abi, Azzedine Alaia, Issey Miyake, Lolita Lempicka and Paule Ka have opened up.

The term *prêt-à-porter* means wearable garments that are partly influenced by haute couture. Bargain hunters will be interested in the *degriffé* offers: reduced brand name clothing from the previous season from which most of the company labels have been removed. A group of shops that also offer outlet items is located on the INSIDER TIP▶ *rue d'Alésia* (152 A6) (*📖 J12*), e.g. Sonja Rykiel (no. 110), Cacharel (no. 114) or Majestic by Chevignon (no. 122). Some labels are marked down by 40 percent or even more during clearance sales.

The Christian Lacroix boutique on rue du Faubourg Saint-Honoré

BIJOUX MONIC (148 A4–5) (*📖 N8*)

The small jewellery store in one of the most lively shopping streets in the Marais district prides itself on its assortment of more than 10,000 pieces of jewellery with prices between 1 and 10,000 euros. *Mon–Sat 10am–7pm, Sun noon–7pm | 5, rue des Francs-Bourgeois | 4th arr. | M 1 Saint-Paul | www.bijouxmonic.com*

CHRISTIAN LOUBOUTIN (155 D4) (*📖 L7*)

The dizzying high heels designed by Christian Louboutin with equally dizzying price tags look their best in the window of the designer's first Parisian boutique. To make sure that your dream shoes don't end in a nightmare, you can INSIDER TIP▶ book a 1.5 hour course on how to walk elegantly in high heels.

See *www.talonsacademy.fr* for dates and locations. *Mon–Sat 10:30am–7pm | rue Jean-Jaques Rousseau | Galerie Véro Dodat | 1st arr. | M 1 Louvre-Rivoli | www.christianlouboutin.com*

COLETTE (146 B3) (*📖 K7*)

Fashion, design and everything that's ultra trendy. If you're looking for something out of the ordinary, you've come to the right place. But the prices are also exceptional – exceptionally high. *213, rue Saint-Honoré | 1st arr. | M 1 Tuileries | www.colette.fr*

DÉPÔT VENTE DE PASSY (144 A5) (*📖 D8*)

The Dépôt sells luxury brands at outlet prices and good bargains are guaranteed. *14, rue de la Tour | 16th arr. | M 6 Trocadéro | www.depot-vente-luxe.fr*

COSMETICS & PERFUME

INSIDER TIP **L'ECLAIREUR**
(147 F5) (*Ø N8*)

The shop has an interesting concept with a mix of object design and names such as Issey Miyake, Prada, Helmut Lange, Comme des Garçons. *3 ter, rue des Rosiers | 4th arr. | M 1 Saint-Paul | www. leclaireur.com*

GERARD DAREL (148 A5) (*Ø N8*)

One of the major affordable French fashion labels for women's clothing. The trousers, dresses and jackets exude a sporty elegance. *41, rue des Francs-Bourgeois | 4th arr. | M 1 Saint Paul | www.gerarddarel. com*

LOW BUDGET

Second-hand: designer clothing in excellent condition but requiring a bit of rummaging – can be found at *Chercheminippes* **(152 A2)** (*Ø J9*). *(102, 109, 110, 111, rue du Cherche-Midi | 6th arr. | M 10 Vaneau |www.chercheminippes.com)*

At *Emmaüs* **(148 C6)** (*Ø P9*) *(Mon 2:30pm–7pm, Tue–Sat 11am–2pm and 2:30–7pm | 54, rue de Charonne | 11th arr. | M 8 Ledru-Rollin |www.emmaus-paris.fr),* the social institution founded by Abbé Pierre, there are bargains galore among second-hand clothing, books, crockery and furniture.

Clearance sales *(soldes)*, which go on for six weeks from the middle of January and from the end of June, are when big-name brands are sold at bargain prices with up to 70 per-cent off.

COSMETICS & PERFUME

DANIEL JOUVENCE (144 C2) (*Ø G6*)

The marine-based cosmetics concern from Brittany advocates beauty and health. Pamper yourself with the extensive array of skincare treatments offered on the lower floor. A fine selection of bath and body products is sold on the ground floor. *91, av. des Champs-Elysées | 8th arr. | M 1, 2, 6 | RER A Charles de Gaulle-Etoile | www.danieljouvance.com*

FRAGONARD (146 B2) (*Ø K5*)

INSIDER TIP The Musée du Parfum *(free admission)* is situated in an opulent Napoleon III-style palais opposite the Opéra Garnier. Across the courtyard is a showroom for the large traditional perfume label Fragonard from Grasse in the South of France. Take a sniff around! *Mon–Sat 9am–6pm, Sun 9:30am–5pm | 9, rue Scribe | 2nd arr. | M 7, 9 Opéra | www.fragonard.com*

SÉPHORA (145 D2) (*Ø G6*)

Giant cosmetic and perfume emporium where makeup is applied nonstop as hot disco rhythms play in the background—for free. The chain store's own brand of bath and body products are both colourful and very pretty. *Mon–Thu 10am–midnight, Fri/Sat 10am–1am | 70–72, av. des Champs-Elysées | 8th arr. | M 1, 2, 6 Charles de Gaulle-Etoile | RER A Charles de Gaulle-Etoile | www.sephora.fr*

ART GALLERIES

The largest assortment of galleries for contemporary art is in the vicinity of the renowned art academy, Beaux Arts, on the *rue de Seine* and its side streets, namely, *rue des Beaux Arts, rue Jacques Callout* and *rue Mazarin* (146 C6) (*Ø K–L8*).

The shops of the cosmetics chain Sephora are bright and eye-catching

A similar cluster of galleries is found on *rue Vieille du Temple* (148 A4–5) (*∭ N7–8*), especially around the Musée Picasso, and on *rue Quincampoix* (147 E4) (*∭ M7*) by the Centre Georges Pompidou.

INSIDER TIP ART GÉNÉRATION
(147 E5) (*∭ M8*)

Paris is known as the city of art. Why not acquire an original as a souvenir? In the vicinity of the Centre Pompidou you can choose from paintings, photographs and graphic art from 25 euros upwards! *Tue–Sat 11am–7:30pm, Sun/Mon 2pm–7:30pm | 67, rue de la Verrerie | 4th arr. | M 1 Hôtel de Ville | www.artgeneration.fr*

VIADUC DES ARTS
(154–155 C–D 2–3) (*∭ O–P 9–10*)

Artists and craftsmen have set up studios beneath the viaduct's 60 brick arches. Equally inspiring cafés and restaurants offer refreshment among the approx. 130 shops. *1–129, av. Daumesnil | 12th arr. | M 1, 5, 8 Bastille | www.leviaducdesarts.com*

MARKETS

Nearly every district in Paris has its "own" market, including some ⊗ *marchés biologiques* – organic markets. For example, *Marché des Batignolles* (140 A5) (*∭ J3–4*) *(Sat 9am–2pm | rue des Batignolles/rue Puteaux | 17th arr. | M 2 Rome)* or *Marché Brancusi* (152 B3) (*∭ K10*) *(Sat 9am–2pm | pl. Constantin Brancusi | 14th arr. | M 4 Vavin)*

MARCHÉ BARBÈS ● (141 E4) (*∭ M3*)

Eclectic Arabian-African bazaar, often very chaotic on account of the low prices. *Wed and Sat mornings | bd. de la Chapelle | 18th arr. | M 2, 4 Barbès-Rochechouart*

INSIDER TIP MARCHÉ BELLEVILLE
(148 C2) (*∭ P5–6*)

The largest, cheapest and most exotic market in Paris is located in the colourful and multicultural district east of the city. *Tue and Fri 7am–2:30pm | 20th arr. | M 2, 11 Belleville | M 2 Menilmontant*

ENTERTAINMENT

CITY **WHERE TO START?**

Paris nightlife is quite lively around the Métro station Bastille, particularly on **rue de Lappe (148 B–C6)** (*∅ O8–9*). Those with more diverse tastes can venture further northeast to **Canal Saint-Martin (148 A–B 1–2)** (*∅ N–O 5–6*), a popular spot for picnics in the evenings, or even further afield to **Belleville (14–149 C–D 1–2)** (*∅ P–Q 5–6*), a former working-class district which is currently very trendy. The more conventional crowd will feel more at ease in the traditional district of **Saint-Germain-des-Prés (146 B–C 5–6)** (*∅ J–K 8–9*).

Parisian nightlife is legendary and thousands of tourists and Parisians alike are out to catch a glimpse of that unique Parisian flair every night.

Whatever is currently considered trendy changes very quickly in Paris. As soon as a district has been discovered by tourists, the Parisian night scene moves elsewhere. The tendency is to migrate further east, where a pub scene has put down roots in the area around the still-affordable artists' flats. Another district that has been *branché* (hip) for some time is Butte-aux-Cailles near the Place d'Italie with its large number of pubs and relatively reasonable prices.

Pleasure-seekers should be aware that public transit operates only until 12:30am (until 2am on Sat), and would be wise to

Bonne soirée:
a night out in Paris requires
money and the proper outfit

consider other return trip options such as night buses, a taxi, or even the first Métro the next morning. Going out for a night on the town in Paris requires proper preparation, especially for nightclubs and discos. Anyone who is not elegantly clad or has an original sense of style has virtually no chance of getting past the unrelenting bouncers. Anyone who hopes to find dance clubs in old warehouses will be disappointed – nearly everything that is cutting-edge is also exclusive. It is also important to budget appropriately: Paris

nightlife is expensive. Cover charges for clubs and discos – depending on the establishment, day of the week and event – can cost between 7 and 20 euros. Incidentally, many locales are closed for the month of August.

BARS

BAR AT THE HOTEL PARTICULIER MONTMARTRE ☀ (148 C4) (*ᗞ K3*)
A favourite among Paris' rich and beautiful crowd. This small hotel is sur-

rounded by a beautiful mature garden, which is perfect for a cocktail. The view of the city from the entrance on the upper slope of Montmartre is fantastic. *Closed Mon | ring the bell on the fence on the small cul-de-sac | 23, av. Junot | 18th arr. | tel. 01 53 41 81 40 | M 12 Lamarck-Caulaincourt | hotel-particuliermontmartre.com*

8th arr. | tel. 01 53 05 90 00 | M 1, 8, 12 Concorde | www.buddhabar.com

CAFÉ BEAUBOURG (147 E5) (*ØJ M7*)
Stylish bar with beautiful terrace directly opposite the Centre Pompidou. Frequented by tourists as well as young Parisians. *Sun–Wed 8am–1am, Thu–Sat 8am–2pm | 43, rue Saint-Merri | 4th arr. | tel. 01 48 87 63 96 | M/RER Châtelet-Les Halles*

Its name is tell-tale: Café Charbon was once a coal merchant's

BARRIO LATINO ★ (154 C1) (*ØJ O9*)
The structure built by Gustave Eiffel is a favourite Parisian entertainment locale. Three storeys with iron balconies surrounding a central atrium with beautiful bar counters. Sofas, Latin music, drinks (good mojitos), tapas and salsa. *Daily | 46, rue du Faubourg Saint-Antoine | 12th arr. | tel. 01 55 78 84 75 | M 8 Ledru-Rollin | M 1, 5, 8 Bastille | www.barrio-latino.com*

BUDDHA BAR (146 A3) (*ØJ J6*)
Bar, restaurant and much more: a true classic. Ethereal ethnic music, Asian cuisine. *Daily | 8/12, rue Boissy d'Anglas |*

CAFÉ CHARBON (148 C3) (*ØJ P6*)
The former coal merchant business from the early 19th century has become an institution. Always full, slow service, but great atmosphere. Small terrace. *Daily (Thu–Sat until 4am) | 109, rue Oberkampf | 11th arr. | tel. 01 43 57 55 13 | M 3 Parmentier*

INSIDER TIP ▶ CHEZ JEANNETTE
(147 E2) (*ØJ M5*)
Comfortable, very popular bistro with funk music and relaxed, friendly atmosphere. *Daily | 47, rue du Faubourg-Saint-Denis | 10th arr. | tel. 01 47 70 30 89 | M 3, 4, 9 Strasbourg-Saint-Denis | www.chezjeannette.com*

CLOSERIE DES LILAS (152 C4) (*ΩΩ K10*)
The former artists' café in Montparnasse is well-known today for its great champagne cocktails and piano music. *Daily noon–1am | 171, bd. de Montparnasse | 6th arr. | tel. 01 40 51 34 50 | M 4 Vavain | RER B Port Royal | www.closeriedeslilas.fr*

INSIDER TIP ▶ FAVELA CHIC
(148 B3) (*ΩΩ O6*)
Brasilian food, good caipirinhas, Latin American rhythms, occasional concerts. Superb atmosphere and always full. *Tue–Sat (Fri/Sat until 4am) | 18, rue du Faubourg du Temple | 11th arr. | tel. 01 40 21 38 14 | M 3, 5, 8, 9, 11 Republique | www.favelachic.com/paris*

LE FUMOIR (147 D4) (*ΩΩ L7*)
Elegant yet very relaxed bar in neo-Colonial style: old time jazz, mahogany interior, a library and good beverages close to the Louvre. With restaurant. *Daily | 6, rue de l'Amiral de Coligny | 1st arr. | tel. 01 42 92 00 24 | M 1 Louvre-Rivoli | www.lefumoir.com*

INSIDER TIP ▶ ICE KUBE BAR
(149 F4) (*ΩΩ N3*)
Paris' one and only ice bar. Drink vodka in the freezing cold as if you were in Russia in winter. But the difference here is that you'll probably only stay for a half an hour! Four vodka cocktails cost 29 euros. *Wed–Sat 7pm–2am | 3, passage Ruelle | 18th arr. | tel. 01 42 05 20 00 | M2 La Chapelle | www.kubehotel-paris.com*

LA PERLE (148 A5) (*ΩΩ N7*)
Super popular and always jam-packed despite its expansion. It is nearly impossible to find a place to sit. This is the place to be seen if you're anybody – or think you are. *Sun–Fri 6am–2am, Sat 8am–2am | 78, rue Vieille-du-Temple | 3rd arr. | tel. 01 42 72 69 93 | M 8 Chemin-Vert | cafelaperle.com*

INSIDER TIP ▶ ROSA BONHEUR
(143 E5) (*ΩΩ Q4*)
Guinguette (open-air café) and trendy bar in the Parc des Buttes-Chaumont with tapas and cocktails, not to men-

---

★ **Barrio Latino**
Three levels for drinking, flirting and dancing → p. 84

★ **Le Batofar**
This barge on the Seine is one of the hottest dance clubs in the city → p. 86

★ **La Casbah**
Disco with an atmosphere from a bygone Arabian era → p. 87

★ **La Dame de Canton**
For a pleasant evening on the Seine → p. 87

★ **Le Carmen**
Exclusive club in Belle-Époque style → p. 87

★ **OPA**
A hotspot for teenagers: dancing and live concerts in a brick loft → p. 87

★ **Rex-Club**
Huge disco and best techno club in Paris → p. 88

★ **New Morning**
The jazz club in Paris, where the best musicians from all over the world make guest performances → p. 89

MARCO POLO HIGHLIGHTS

tion the most gorgeous sunset in Paris. *Wed–Sun until midnight | 2, av. de la Cascade | 19th arr. | Entrance after 8pm: large gate opposite rue Botzaris 74 | tel. 01 42 00 00 45 | M 7 Botzaris | www.rosa bonheur.fr*

INSIDER TIP WANDERLUST
(154 B3) (*∅ O11*)

This new hip location with a terrace on the Seine is a restaurant, concert hall, gallery and club in one. Yoga and knitting courses plus other activities are offered on weekends. *Thu–Sat noon–5am, Sun noon–7pm | 32, quai d'Austerlitz | 13th arr. | tel. 01 70 74 41 74 | M 7, 10 Gare d'Austerlitz | www.wanderlustparis.com*

CLUBS & DISCOS

LE BALAJO (140 B6) (*∅ O8*)

The Balajo is Paris' long-time salsa temple situated in the heart of the Bastille district. If you're game, learn a nostalgic drawing room dance at tea time on Monday afternoons between 2pm and 7pm. *Tue–Sun | 9, rue de Lappe | 11th arr. | tel. 01 47 00 07 87 | M 1, 5, 8 Bastille | www. balajo.fr*

INSIDER TIP BARON SAMEDI
(148 B2) (*∅ O6*)

Old concert posters from Ray Charles, Marvin Gaye and others hang on the walls. In the concert room you can hear Rhythm & Blues or Funk, next to it is a dance floor with a big TV screen showing concerts. Very trendy. *Mon–Sat until 2am | 12, rue des Goncourt | 11th arr. | tel. 01 42 77 16 03 | M 11 Goncourt | www. aubaronsamedi.fr*

LE BATOFAR ★
(154 C5) (*∅ P11*)

The red barge in front of the Bibliothèque Nationale de France is one of the most popular meeting places in Paris. Experimental and techno music: very *branché*. Terrace on the deck. Quite affordable. *Tue, Thu–Sat| 11, quai Francois-Mauriac | 13th arr. | tel. 09 71 25 50 61 | M 6 Quai de la Gare | www.batofar.org*

INTO THE EARLY HOURS

For a metropolis such as Paris there are relatively few places where you can get a drink or snack in the early hours. Classics include: *Le Grand Café* **(146 B2)** (*∅ K6*) *(24 hours | 4, bd. des Capucines | 9. arr. | M 3, 7, 8 Opéra | RER A Auber | www.legrandcafe.com)*, a very popular, large brasserie.
La Mercerie **(148 C3)** (*∅ P6*) *(24 hours | 98, rue Oberkampf | 11th arr. | M3 Parmentier)* in one of the trendy districts.
Au Pied de Cochon **(147 D4)** (*∅ L7*) *(24 hours | 6, rue Coquillère | 1st arr. | M/ RER: Châtelet-Les Halles | www.piedde cochon.com)*.
Chez Denise **(147 D4)** (*∅ L7*) *(Mon– Fri 24 hours | 5, rue des Prouvaires | 1st arr. | M 1 Louvre-Rivoli)* serves traditional cuisine.
La Maison de l'Aubrac **(145 D2)** (*∅ G6*) *(24 hours | 37, rue Marbeuf | 8th arr. | M 1, 9 Franklin D. Roosevelt | www.maison-aubrac.com)*.
Le Dépanneur **(140 C5)** (*∅ K4*) *(24 hours | 27, rue Fontaine | 9th arr. | M 2, 12 Pigalle | M 2 Blanche | ledepanneur pigalle.com)*.

Le Batofar: the deck-turned-dance floor on the barge rocks night after night

LE CARMEN ⭐ (140 C5) (📖 K4)

If you are not a fan of snobs, avoid this club! But, if you do give it a chance, you'll be more than impressed by the former residence of the composer Georges Bizet with its huge mirrors, tall columns and ornate ceiling. *Daily 10pm–5am | 34, rue Duperré | 9th arr. | tel. 0145 26 50 00 | M2 Blanche | www.le-carmen.fr*

LA CASBAH ⭐
(155 D1) (📖 P9)

This popular disco has an Arabian Nights flair and a restaurant. Sometimes belly dancing is offered. *Mon–Sat, Club 11pm–5am | 18–20, rue de la Forge-Royale | 11th arr. | tel. 0143 71 04 39 | M 8 Faidherbe-Chaligny | www.casbah.fr*

LA DAME DE CANTON ⭐
(154 C5) (📖 P12)

The Chinese junk anchored in front of the National Library was known for years as the "Guinguette Pirate". Concerts, lots of Salsa music and a restaurant. *Tue–Sat | Port de la gare | 13th arr. | tel. 0153 61 08 49 | M 6 Quai de la Gare | M 14 Bibliothèque F. Mitterrand | www.damedecanton.com*

LE DIVAN DU MONDE (140 C5) (📖 L4)

The old Paris Theatre with a stage and gallery in the vibrant Pigalle district now offers interesting concerts and music by DJs (Funk, Reggae, etc.). With restaurant. *Daily (Fri/Sat until 6am) | 75, rue des Martyrs | 18th arr. | tel. 0140 05 06 99 | M 1 Pigalle | www.divandumonde.com*

OPA ⭐
(148 B6) (📖 O9)

Bar, club and concert venue. Rock, funk and house music flow through the brick lofts. Concerts on most Wednesdays and Thursdays, but dancing until the break of dawn on weekends. *Tue–Thu, Sun 8pm–2am, Fri/Sat 9pm–6am | 9, rue Biscornet | 12th arr. | tel. 0146 28 12 90 | M 1, 5, 8, Bastille | www.opa-paris.com*

JAZZ & LIVE MUSIC

LE QUEEN (145 D2) *(𝄢 G6)*
The year-long No. 1 address with a gay and hetero clientele. An eclectic agenda every day. *Daily | 102, av. des Champs-Elysées | 8th arr. | tel. 01 92 70 73 30 | M 1 George V | www.queen.fr*

REX-CLUB ⭐ (147 D2) *(𝄢 M6)*
A huge disco under the cinema complex. Best techno club in the city, also house, disco, concerts. *Wed–Sat from 11pm | 5, bd. Poissonière | 2nd arr. | tel. 01 42 36 10 96 | M 8, 9 Bonne Nouvelle | www.rexclub.com*

LOW BUDGET

Every Friday evening thousands of ● inline skaters congregate on a nearly 20 mile-long stretch of roads closed off to traffic. Start is at 10pm between Montparnasse station and the Montparnasse tower **(151 F3)** *(𝄢 H–J 10–11)* (*Gare Montparnasse | 6th arr. | M 4, 6, 12, 13 Montparnasse-Bienvenue | www.pari-roller.com*).

The old-fashioned atmosphere of the tiny bar/restaurant ● *Le Limonaire* **(139 D2)** *(𝄢 L5)* (*daily from 8:15pm, restaurant; free shows from 10pm | 18, cité Bergére | 9th arr. | tel. 01 45 23 33 33 |M 8, 9 Grands-Boulevards | limonaire.free.fr*) is the perfect stage for chansons and cabarets.

The *Flèche d'Or* **(149 F6)** *(𝄢 S8)* (*daily from 8:45pm, Thu–Sat until 5am | free admission | 102, rue de Bagnolet | 20th arr. | tel. 01 44 64 01 02 | M 2 Alexandre Dumas | www.flechedor.fr*) is a truly fashionable meeting place located in a former station: concerts (techno to jazz), cabarets, bar and a disco.

INSIDER TIP ▶ SHOWCASE
(145 E3) *(𝄢 H7)*
The former boathouse under the arches of the glimmering gold Pont Alexandre III has sprung to life at weekends. The city's new "in" nightclub. Occasional concerts. *Daily | Port des Champs-Elysées/rive droite | 8th arr. | tel. 01 45 61 25 43 | M 1, 13 Champs-Elysées-Clemenceau | www.showcase.fr*

SOCIAL CLUB (147 D2) *(𝄢 L5)*
Temple of the electro and techno scene in an old printing shop with a loft atmosphere. Fantastic concerts. *Wed–Sat from 11pm | 142, rue Montmartre | 2nd arr. | tel. 01 40 28 05 55 | M 3 Bourse | M 3, 8 Grands-Boulevards | www.parissocialclub.com*

JAZZ & LIVE MUSIC

LE BAISER SALÉ (147 E5) *(𝄢 M8)*
Jazz club with a large bar and jazz videos. Relaxed atmosphere with salsa, blues, fusion and funk music. *Daily | 58, rue des Lombards | 1st arr. | tel. 01 42 33 37 71 | M/RER Châtelet-Les Halles | www.lebaisersale.com*

LE BATACLAN (148 B4) *(𝄢 O7)*
Legendary Paris concert and show stage hosting French and international stars. Closed until further notice after the terrorist attacks of 13 November 2015. *50, bd. Voltaire | 11th arr. | tel. 01 43 14 00 30 | M 5, 9 Oberkampf | www.le-bataclan.com*

LA BELLEVILLOISE (149 E3) *(𝄢 R6)*
An old hall from the 19th century with a wonderful potpourri of activity: live concerts, art exhibitions and assorted events plus a café and restaurant. *Wed–Fri 6pm–2am, Sat/Sun 11am–2am | 19, rue Boyer | 20th arr. | tel. 01 46 36 07 07 | M 3 Gambetta | www.labellevilloise.com*

Crazy Horse: striptease with a twist – a colourful and imaginative combination of the erotic and aesthetic

CAVEAU DE LA HUCHETTE
(147 D6) (*L9*)

The old walls of a medieval vaulted cellar come to life every evening with live jazz music. *Daily | 5, rue de la Huchette | 5th arr. | tel. 01 43 26 65 05 | M 4 Saint-Michel, Cité | www.caveaudelahuchette.fr*

AU DUC DES LOMBARDS
(147 E5) (*M8*)

Easy-going club highlighting a wide spectrum of music, from free jazz to hard bop. The restaurant (Tue–Sat) serves small meals. *Mon–Sat | 42, rue des Lombards | 1st arr. | tel. 01 42 33 22 88 | M/RER Châtelet-Les Halles | www.ducdeslombards.com*

NEW MORNING ★ (147 E1) (*M5*)

The city's best and most famous jazz club where renowned international musicians take the stage. *Daily until the early morning | 7–9, rue des Petites-Ecuries | 10th arr. | tel. 01 45 23 51 41 | M 4 Château d'Eau | www.newmorning.com*

LE PETIT JOURNAL MONTPARNASSE
(151 F4) (*J11*)

One of the most important jazz clubs in the city. *Daily | 13, rue du Commandant René Mouchotte | 14th arr. | tel. 01 43 21 56 70 | M 4, 6, 12, 13 Montparnasse-Bienvenüe | petitjournalmontparnasse.com*

CABARETS & REVUES

LE CRAZY HORSE (144 C3) (*F6*)

Eroticism paired with artistic sensibility. A combination of ballet and striptease with beautiful aesthetic effects. *Shows: Sun–Fri 8:15pm, 10:45pm, Sat 7pm, 9:30pm, 11:45pm | prices, with or without meal, vary | 12, av. George V | 8th arr. | tel. 01 47 23 32 32 | M 1 George V | M 9 Alma Marceau | www.lecrazyhorseparis.com*

AU LAPIN AGILE (141 D3) (*L3*)

Many well-known poets and painters once frequented this picturesque Montmartre cabaret founded in 1860. A great vibe, you'll wish you were fluent in the language. *Tue–Sun 9pm–2am | 28 euros (includes a beverage) | 22, rue des Saules | 18th arr. | tel. 01 46 06 85 87 | M 12 Lamarck-Coulaincourt | www.au-lapin-agile.com*

LE LIDO DE PARIS (144 C2) (*Ø F5*)

Spectacular productions with an American flair plus a restaurant whose quality has vastly improved over the years. *Daily 9am–2pm, shows between 1pm and 11pm | from 115 euros (incl. half a bottle of champagne) | 116bis, av. des Champs-Elysées | 8th arr. | tel. 01 40 76 56 10 | M 1 George V | www.lido.fr*

LE MOULIN ROUGE (140 B4) (*Ø K3*)

Lavish revues in the "red mill" immortalised by Henri de Toulouse-Lautrec and the birthplace of the cancan, located at the foot of Montmartre. *Shows between 1pm and 11pm | 110 euros (including half a bottle of champagne), with meal from 165 euros | 82, bd. de Clichy | 18th arr. | tel. 01 53 09 82 82 | M 2 Blanche | www. moulinrouge.fr*

CINEMA

Paris has more than 300 cinemas. Foreign films, as a rule, are shown in their original language with French subtitles – *v. o. (version originale)* – while films dubbed into French are denoted as *v. f. (version française)*. Main showings begin between 7:30pm and 8:30pm. Admission is usually between 8 and 10 euros, but many cinemas offer discounts on Mondays.

CINÉMATHÈQUE FRANÇAISE

(155 D4) (*Ø P11*)

The futuristic building by the architect Frank O. Gehry houses the Cinémathèque offering a selection of 40,000 films and extensive archives. Various cinemas with interesting, often rare screenings. *Closed Tue | 51, rue de Bercy | 12th arr. |*

tel. 01 71 19 33 33 | M 6, 14 Bercy | www. cinematheque.fr

MK2

(154 C5) (*Ø P12*)

Ultramodern, elongated, dazzling white multiplex with 14 cinemas in the futuristic surroundings of the "Très Grande Bibliothèque". *128/162 av. de France | 13th arr. | tel. 08 92 69 84 84 | M 14 Bibliothèque François Mitterrand | RER C Bibliothèque François Mitterrand | www. mk2.com*

INSIDER TIP ▶ LA PAGODE

(145 F6) (*Ø H9*)

Lovely Chinese-Japanese pagoda from the end of the 19th century with a tiled façade and Japanese décor in the auditorium. In the summer, enjoy the "salon de thé" in the garden surrounded by bamboo shoots and bronze lions. *57bis, rue de Babylone | 7th arr. | tel. 01 45 55 48 48 | M 13 Saint-Francois Xavier*

CONCERTS

A number of stages showcase all types of music by top performers and amateurs alike. The city is also an important venue for ethnic music from all over the world. Especially during the summer, there are many free events and musicians often play in the parks in July/August.

LA CIGALE (140 C5) (*Ø L4*)

International stars have performed at this venue, including Kevin Costner and his band, Modern West. *120, bd. Rochechouart | 18th arr. | tel. 01 49 25 89 99 | M 2, 12 Pigalle | www.lacigale.fr*

OLYMPIA (145 B2) (*Ø J6*)

Legendary, world-famous concert hall hosting performers ranging from French celebrities to the Rolling Stones.

28, bd. des Capucines | 9th arr. | tel. 08 92 68 33 68 | M 3, 7, 8 Opéra | RER A Auber | www.olympiahall.com

LE ZÉNITH (143 E2) *(Ⓜ R2)*
This huge concert hall in the Parc de la Villette is a venue for rock and pop concerts. *211, av. Jean-Jaurès | 19th arr. | tel.*

The MK2 Odéon in Saint-Germain-des-Prés is one of over 300 cinemas in Paris

INSIDER TIP ▶ PHILHARMONIE DE PARIS (151 F3) *(Ⓜ R2)*
Construction on the philharmonic hall designed by Jean Novel with its spectacular architecture including an accessible roof was completed in 2015. None of the over 2,400 seats is more than 30 m (33 yds) from the stage in the middle. The repertoire ranges from classic to world music and there is a café. *221, av. Jean-Jaurès | tel. 01 44 84 44 84 | www.philharmoniedeparis.fr | M 5 Porte de Pantin*

THÉÂTRE DU CHÂTELET (147 D5) *(Ⓜ L8)*
One of the most magnificent auditoriums in Paris where classical concerts are often held. *1, pl. du Châtelet | 4th arr. | tel. 01 40 28 28 28 | M/RER: Châtelet-Les Halles | www.chatelet-theatre.com*

01 44 52 54 56 | M 5 Porte de Pantin | www.zenith-paris.com

THEATRE

Grand-scale theatrical productions are rare in Paris. Visitors to Paris with a good command of French can nevertheless find a number of theatrical highlights such as Peter Brooks' *Les Bouffes du Nord* (www.bouffesdunord.com) or the *Comédie Française (www.comedie-francaise.fr)*.

THÉÂTRE DE LA VILLE (147 D5) *(Ⓜ L8)*
The premier stage in Paris for modern dance, but also a venue for dramatic works and music (especially ethnic). *2, pl. du Châtelet | 4th arr. | tel. 01 42 74 22 77 | M/RER Châtelet-Les Halles | www.theatredelaville-paris.com*

WHERE TO STAY

As one of the most important tourist spots worldwide, Paris has an extensive range of accommodation in every category.

In addition to the globally recognised hotel palaces such as the Plaza Athénée, which are synonymous with luxury and sophistication, there are also real jewels among the more reasonable, modest establishments; you just have to know where to find them. Many offer authentic charm, an informal atmosphere and are lovingly maintained. These addresses, as well as certain luxury hotels, are booked up quickly from April to July, as well as in September and October. It is advisable to reserve your hotel of choice well in advance. If you're pressed for time, the Office du Tourisme (see p. 126) can lend a hand. Hotel reservations can also be made at: *www.leshotelsde paris.com*.

The hotel category (one to four stars) is shown on hotel signs. Note, however, there are also hotels that are not classified, and the number of stars is not always indicative of the amenities provided.

Most places demand written confirmation by e-mail, fax, letter or a voucher. A credit card number or a deposit is also often required. Cancellations must be made in writing. Rates tend to vary according to the season and, as a rule, room prices quoted in brochures and price lists apply to a double room without breakfast. In Paris, a nominal visitor's tax is charged. To avoid misun-

Bonne nuit: a large selection of accommodation guarantees a restful night in Paris – in all price categories

derstandings, check the price list beforehand which has to be clearly displayed at the hotel entrance.

HOTELS: EXPENSIVE

FOUR SEASONS GEORGE V
(144 C2) (*ℳ F6*)

After extensive restorations in the 18th-century style, this prestigious address is more radiant than ever with its generously sized, luxurious rooms and *Le Cinq*, Philippe Legendre's two-

star restaurant. *184 rooms, 61 suites | 31, av. George V | 8th arr. | tel. 01 49 52 70 00 | M 1 George V | www. fourseasons.com*

L'HÔTEL ★ ●
(146 C5) (*ℳ K8*)

Highly distinguished but nevertheless quite cosy, and more beautiful than ever following its tasteful renovations by the famous designer Jacques Garcia. Even the renowned writer Oscar Wilde, who died here in 1900 in suite no. 13, appreciated the hotel's comfort. Unique round atrium. Large rooms in the Baroque, Empire, Art Deco or Japanese style. The vaulted cellar has a swimming pool and hamam reminiscent of a Roman spa. Incredible Michelin-star restaurant *(Le Bélier)*. *16 rooms, 4 suites |*

The cosy hotel with the famous name is *très charmant*

13, rue des Beaux Arts | 6th arr. | tel. 01 44 41 99 00 | M 4 Saint-Germain-des-Prés | www.l-hotel.com

K+K HOTEL CAYRÉ (146 A5) *(𝖒 J10)*

This boutique hotel combines exceptional comfort and modern design. The chain, which has established hotels in various European cities, maintains an excellent standard at attractive prices. In Paris, the hotel is optimally located in Saint-Germain-des-Prés. *125 rooms and suites | 4, bd. Raspail | 7th arr. | tel. 01 45 44 38 88 | M 12 Rue du Bac | www.kkhotels.com/cayre*

MURANO (148 B4) *(𝖒 O7)*

Hotel with an ultramodern vibe, decorated almost entirely in white. Two suites have their own pool, some suites have a terrace. *51 rooms and suites | 13, bd. du Temple | 3rd arr. | tel. 01 42 71 20 00 | M 8 Filles du Calvaire | www.murano resort.com*

PAVILLON DE LA REINE (148 B5) *(𝖒 O8)*

You'll feel very regal when you pass through the arcades to the former royal square, the Place des Vosges, leaving the hectic Marais district behind you as you enter this peaceful oasis with its lush courtyard. The spa is utterly relaxing. *41 rooms, 16 suites | 28, pl. des Vosges | 3rd arr. | tel. 01 40 29 19 19 | M 1, 5, 8 Bastille | www.pavillon-de-la-reine.com*

TERRASS" HÔTEL ⚘ (148 B4) *(𝖒 K3)*

This hotel lies at the foot of Montmarte. It owes its name to its 1,500 square-foot rooftop terrace offering a truly fantastic view over the entire city. All 92 rooms were stylishly renovated in 2015. *12–14, rue Joseph de Maistre | 18th arr. | tel. 01 46 06 72 88 | M 12 Abbesses | www.terrass-hotel.com*

HOTELS: MODERATE

HÔTEL DES ARTS (147 D2) *(𝖒 L5)*

Charming and lovely small hotel in a quiet yet central location with spacious rooms.

25 rooms | 7, cité Bergère | 9th arr. | tel. 01 42 46 73 30 | M 8, 9 Grands Boulevards | www.hoteldesarts.fr

HÔTEL ARVOR SAINT GEORGES
(140 C6) (*M K4*)

Well maintained, renovated hotel in a quiet neighbourhood. Modern design. Not far from the Gare du Nord, Montmartre and major department stores. *31 rooms, 5 suites | 8, rue Laferrière | 9th arr. | tel. 01 48 78 60 92 | M 12 Saint-Georges | hotelarvor.com*

HÔTEL DE L'AVRE
(150 C2) (*M F9*)

This small hotel near the École Militaire is full of charm. The pastel-coloured rooms have all been designed with the utmost care. In summer you can have breakfast in the lovely courtyard garden. *26 rooms | 21, rue de l'Avre | 15th arr. | tel. 01 45 75 31 03 | M 6, 8, 10 La Motte-Picquet Grenelle | www.hotel delavre.com*

HÔTEL CHOPIN
(147 D2) (*M L6*)

Small, but charming hotel in a beautiful 19th-century building at the end of the lovely Passage Jouffroy (no. 46). Pleasantly quiet. *36 rooms | 10, bd. Montmartre | 9th arr. | tel. 01 47 70 58 10 | M 8, 9 Grands Boulevards | www.hotel-chopin.fr*

HÔTEL DU COLLÈGE DE FRANCE
(153 D1) (*M L9*)

This cosy and well-run hotel is situated in the centre of the hectic Quartier Latin in a surprisingly quiet location. *29 rooms | 7, rue Thénard | 5th arr. | tel. 01 43 26 78 36 | M 10 Saint-Michel | RER B Saint-Michel | www.hotel-collegedefrance.com*

HÔTEL DES GRANDES ECOLES ★
(153 E2) (*M M9*)

An absolute highlight. Who would expect a country house with park-like grounds only a stone's throw from the vibrant rue Mouffetard and Panthéon? Each room in the three small buildings is decorated with period furniture. Most rooms have a view of the garden where you can enjoy breakfast in this peaceful setting. *51 rooms | 75, rue du Cardinal Lemoine | 5th arr. | tel. 01 43 26 79 23 | M 10 Cardinal Lemoine | www.hotel-grandes-ecoles.com*

HÔTEL LANGLOIS ★ (140 C6) (*M K5*)

A real gem. The elegant entrance hall decorated with marble and wood lives up to its promise. The 24 rooms and three suites are individually furnished with original Art

---

★ L'Hôtel
This jewel offers the most exclusive rooms and a pool in a vaulted cellar → p. 93

★ Hôtel des Grandes Ecoles
A country house and garden in the heart of Paris → p. 95

★ Hôtel Langlois
Marble busts and Art Deco, Art Nouveau and a fireplace in every room → p. 95

★ Hôtel de Nesle
Oasis of calm in lively Saint-Germain-des-Prés → p. 98

★ Nouvel Hôtel
Cosy and cheerful with a Provence-style garden → p. 99

MARCO POLO HIGHLIGHTS

HOTELS: MODERATE

Deco and Art Nouveau furniture. ❧ Stellar view of Sacré-Cœur. Fireplace in each room. 63, *rue Saint-Lazare | 9th arr. | tel. 01 48 74 78 24 | M 12 Trinité d'Estienne d'Orves | www.hotel-langlois.com*

HÔTEL MOLIÈRE (146 C3) (⑪ K7)
This enchanting hotel is located on the street where the great playwright was born in 1622 and is only steps away from the Palais Royal. It is no surprise that the hotel exudes Old French elegance. *32 rooms | 21, rue Molière | 1st arr. | tel. 01 42 96 22 01 | M 1 Palais Royal-Musée du Louvre | www.hotel-moliere.fr*

LE RELAIS DU MARAIS (147 F3) (⑪ N6)
Two-star hotel with elegant furnishings in the middle of Marais. Close to the best places for shopping. Unusually large breakfast buffet. *36 rooms | 76, rue Turbigo | 3rd arr. | tel. 01 42 72 78 88 | M 3, 11 Arts et Métiers | www.hotel-paris-relaisdumarais.com*

HÔTEL SAINT-CHARLES
(153 E6) (⑪ M12)
A recently renovated, very attractive designer hotel in the heart of the lively nightlife district Butte-aux-Cailles. Pleasantly calm despite its location and with

LUXURY HOTELS

Le Bristol (145 E2) (⑪ H5)
The very elegant luxury palace on the haute couture mile rue du Faubourg Saint-Honoré has welcomed its illustrious guests since 1925. Alongside a wonderful spa and the three star restaurant *Epicure,* it also has an enchanting French-style garden. From 850 euros. *188 rooms and suites | 112, rue du Faubourg Saint-Honoré | 8th arr. | tel. 01 53 43 43 00 | M 9 Miromesnil | www. lebristolparis.com*

Fouquet's Barrière (146 A3) (⑪ F6)
No expense has been spared since this first luxury hotel in Paris was built in 1928. Black marble from China and white marble from Carrara, the finest materials, suites as large as 1700 ft^2 as well as a huge spa area, all located directly on the Champs-Elysées. From 710 euros. *107 rooms and suites | 47, av. George V | 8th arr. | tel. 01 40 69 60 00 | M 1 George V | www. fouquets-barriere.com*

Plaza Athénée (145 D3) (⑪ G6)
The epitome of a Parisian palais hotel situated on the same street as the great fashion designers caters to celebrities. Gorgeous courtyard, beautiful rooms in the classical and Art Deco styles. The hotel is also home to Alain Ducasse's three-star restaurant and a very trendy bar. From 740 euros. *143 rooms, 45 suites | 25, av. Montaigne | 8th arr. | tel. 01 53 67 66 65 | M 1, 9 Franklin D. Roosevelt | www.plaza-athenee-paris.com*

Shangri-La (144 B3) (⑪ F7)
The hotel chain from Hong Kong has established a fantastic five-star hotel in Europe for the first time, which boasts a prime location in Paris. Some of the ❧ rooms in this palatial hotel have a breathtaking view of the nearby Eiffel Tower. From 750 euros. *80 rooms and suites | 10, av d'Iéna | 16th arr. | tel. 01 53 67 19 98 | M 9 Iéna | www.shangri-la.com*

The restaurant in the Le Bistrol is just as elegantly decorated as the rest of the hotel

a nice atmosphere. *60 rooms | 6, rue de l'Espérance | 13th arr. | tel. 01 45 89 56 54 | M 6 Corvisart, M 5, 6, 7 Place d'Italie | www.hotel-saint-charles.com*

HÔTEL SAINT-MERRY
(147 E5) (*ɯ M8*)

Unconventional hotel that was once part of a Gothic chapel and now furnished accordingly. Its location between Les Halles and Marais is ideal for tourists. *11 rooms (10 with bath/WC) | 78, rue de la Verrerie | 4th arr. | tel. 01 42 78 14 15 | M 1: Hôtel de Ville | www.saint merrymarais.com*

HOTELS: BUDGET

HÔTEL DES ARTS-MONTMARTRE
(140 C4) (*ɯ K3*)

Renoir painted his famous painting, *Moulin de la Galette,* only a few feet from here. The hotel is located on a quiet lane that winds up Montmartre. The 50 rooms are tastefully furnished. Surprisingly affordable for a three-star hotel. *78, rue Tholozé | 18th arr. | tel. 01 46 06 30 52 | M 2 Blanche | www.arts-hotel-paris.com*

INSIDER TIP ▶ HÔTEL ELDORADO
(140 A4) (*ɯ J3*)

A real treasure. A small Chinese junk in a lovely garden at the centre of Paris with individually furnished rooms in African or Asian style. Quiet, but centrally located at the foot of Montmartre. Great wine bar and restaurant with a summer terrace, cuisine with a Mediterranean flair. *39 rooms | 18, rue des Dames | 17th arr. | tel. 01 45 22 35 21 | M 2, 13 Place de Clichy | eldorado.fr*

ERMITAGE SACRÉ-CŒUR 🌿
(141 D4) (*ɯ L3*)

This very pretty romantic little hotel in a beautiful palais from the time of Napoleon III is located in the middle of the Montmatre quarter. Tranquil with a great view of the city. Breakfast is in-

vaulted cellar provides a suitable alternative. Not far from the main attractions. The narrow corridors seem rather austere, but

The Jardin de Villiers is one of the few Paris hotels with a garden

cluded. *5 rooms, 1 suite, 1 apt. | 24, rue Lamarck | 18th arr. | tel. 01 42 64 79 22 | M 4 Château Rouge | www.ermitagesa crecoeur.fr*

HÔTEL HENRI IV
(147 D5) *(J8)*

Very affordable small hotel on a beautiful, tree-lined square in the middle of the Île de la Cité. Simple, bright rooms in a very quiet neighbourhood. *20 rooms | 25, pl. Dauphine | 1st arr. | tel. 01 43 54 44 53 | M 7 Pont Neuf | www.henri4hotel.fr*

HÔTEL JARDIN DE VILLIERS
(139 E5) *(H3)*

Pleasant small hotel with – as its name suggests – an attractive garden where you can enjoy breakfast. On rainy days the

the rooms are quite modern and tastefully furnished. *26 rooms | 18, rue Claude Pouillet | 17th arr. | tel. 01 42 67 15 60 | M 2, 3 Villiers | www.jardindevilliers.com*

HÔTEL DE NESLE ★
(146 C6) *(L8)*

You'll be transported into another world as soon as you see the entrance hall with its flea market treasures. The romantic rooms are decorated very individually, each one different, and many inspired by Molière plays. Some do not have their own bath/WC. There is even a Moroccan room INSIDER TIP (with a real hamam), an Egyptian, a Provençal and an African room. Exquisite garden with sculptures and terrace. *20 rooms | 7, rue de Nesle | 6th arr. | tel. 01 43 54 62 41 |*

M 4, 10 Odéon | www.hoteldenesleparis.com

NOUVEL HÔTEL ⭐
(155 F2) (𝄞 *R10*)

Lovingly furnished, very quiet and clean rooms with Laura Ashley décor. Each room has a refurbished bathroom and a TV. Informal atmosphere. The small Provence-inspired courtyard and beautiful, luxuriant garden of wild vines and bamboo is the ideal place to relax. Room 109 with its direct access to the garden is extremely popular. Two family rooms and a three-bed room are also available. *27 rooms | 24, av. du Bel-Air | 12th arr. | tel. 01 43 43 01 81 | M 1, 2, 6, 9 Nation | RER A | www.nouvel-hotel-paris.com*

INSIDER TIP ◗ OOPS! HOSTEL
(153 E5) (𝄞 *M12*)

Trendy design hotel for young people on a budget. Great location for exploring Paris with a Vélib station right in front of the entrance. Five minutes from rue Mouffetard. *30 double and shared rooms | 50, av. des Gobelins | 13th arr. | tel. 01 47 07 47 00 | M 7 Les Gobelins | www.oops-paris.com*

HÔTEL PRATIC
(148 A6) (𝄞 *N8*)

Well-looked after, quaint hotel with charm and old furniture at the heart of the Marais district and close to Place des Vosges. *23 rooms | 9, rue d'Ormesson | 4th arr. | tel. 01 48 87 80 47 | M 1 Saint-Paul | www.pratichotelparis.com*

HÔTEL DU PRINTEMPS
(155 F2) (𝄞 *R10*)

Well-kept, quiet, good-value hotel that has recently been tastefully renovated. Rooms with four beds available for families. *38 rooms | 80, bd. de Picpus |*

12th arr. | tel. 01 43 43 62 31 | M 6 Picpus | www.hotel-paris-printemps.com

SOLAR HÔTEL ◉
(152 B5) (𝄞 *J12*)

The Solar is the first hotel in Paris to call itself ecological and not only publicly divulges how much energy it uses, but also endeavours to reduce this figure. Breakfast is 100% organic. Nobody will mind if you bring your own food to eat in the garden. True to form, bicycles are at your disposal for exploring the city. *24 rooms | 22, rue Boulard | 14th arr. | tel. 01 43 21 08 20 | M 6 Denfert-Rochereau | RER B Denfert-Rochereau | www.solarhotel.fr*

LOW BUDGET

MIJE (tel. 01 42 74 23 45 | www.mije.com) runs three outstanding youth hostels in beautifully renovated city palais from the 16th and 17th century in the middle of the Marais district in the 4th arrondission **(147 F6)** (𝄞 *N8*). They are located at *6, rue de Fourcy (M 1 Saint-Paul), 11, rue du Fauconnier (M 1 Saint-Paul)* and *12, rue des Barres (M 1, 11 Hôtel de Ville)*. Guests can enjoy an inexpensive meal in the adjoining restaurant on rue de Fourcy.

One of the cheapest hotels in the centre of Paris is the *Hôtel Tiquetonne* **(147 E3)** (𝄞 *L7*) *(48 rooms | 6, rue Tiquetonne | 2th arr. | tel. 01 42 36 94 58 | M 4 Etienne Marcel | www.hoteltiquetonne.fr)*. Quiet location (pedestrian zone) in the lively quarter around Les Halles. Great value for money.

HOTEL BOOKING SERVICES

HOTEL BOOKING SERVICES

OFFICE DU TOURISME

(146 C3) (*Ⅲ K6*)

The tourist office provides assistance in booking private rooms, flats and so-called "hotel residences" equipped with kitchens for large numbers of guests. *Mon–Sat 10am–7pm, Sun 9am–7pm | 25, rue des Pyramides | 1st arr. | tel. 08 92 68 30 00 (*) | M 7, 14 Pyramides | RER A Auber | www.parisinfo.com*

BED & BREAKFAST

More and more tourists are renting rooms or flats from locals. A holiday flat is a cost-saving measure for families in particular because meals can be made at home. The website *www.bed-and-breakfast-in-paris.com* has plenty of information on bed-and-breakfasts in Paris. Another advantage to this type of accommodation is the chance to get to know your surroundings and the people from a local point-of-view and to improve your language skills.

YOUTH HOSTELS

AUBERGE DE JEUNESSE ADVENIAT

(145 D2) (*Ⅲ G6*)

New, uncharacteristically chic youth hostel in the equally chic district close to the Champs-Elysées. A hostel card can be obtained locally – and there is no age restriction. The facility is managed by the Catholic church and closes between 11am and 4pm. *10, rue François-1er | 8th arr. | tel. 01 77 45 89 10 | M 1,*

HORSES – FOOTBALL – TENNIS

The French are passionate about all types of horse racing. There are several racetracks in Paris and the surrounding area. Info: *www.france-galop.com*. The three most important venues are *Auteuil* **(156 A4)** (*Ⅲ A–B 8–9*) *(route des Lacs à Passy | M 10 Porte d'Auteuil)*; *Saint-Cloud* **(158 B4)** (*Ⅲ 0*) *(1, rue du Camp Canadien | tram 2 Suresnes Longchamp)* and *Longchamp* **(158 A4)** (*Ⅲ 0*) *(Bois de Boulogne | route des Tribunes | M 10 Porte d'Auteuil | shuttle bus)*. Up to 30,000 visitors go to Longchamp on the first weekend in October for the Prix de l'Arc de Triomphe. Info: *www.prixarcdetriomphe.com*. The trotting race, Prix d'Amérique in the *Hippodrome de Vincennes* **(159 D4)** (*Ⅲ 0*) *(2, route de la Ferme | RER A Joinville Le Pont)*, takes place on the last Sunday in January. Info: *www.hippodrome-vincennes.com*.

Now that the football club *Paris-Saint-Germain (PSG) (www.psg.fr)* has once again become a top European team, the stadum is worth a visit. PSG play in the *Parc des Princes* **(158 B4)** (*Ⅲ 0*) *(rue du Commandant Guilbaud | 16th arr. | M 9, 10, 22 Porte de Saint-Cloud)*. Every May/June, one of the world's largest tennis tournaments is held at Roland Garros. Tickets (up to mid-March) via *www.frenchopen.org* or *www.rolandgarros.com*. A small reserve is sold at the *Stade Roland-Garros* **(156 A4)** (*Ⅲ A10*) itself. *(2, av. Cordon Bennett | 16th arr. | M 9, 10, 22 Porte de Saint-Cloud or Porte d'Auteuil)*.

At least as beautiful as home sweet home: holiday flats in Paris

M 13 Champs-Elysées-Clemenceau | www. adveniat-paris.org

AUBERGES DE JEUNESSE PARIS – YVES ROBERT ⊙ (150 A4) *(🕮 N3)*

This tastefully-furnished and environmentally-friendly hostel, outfitted with solar panels on the roof, opened at the end of 2013. The former railway station halls have been converted into 103 rooms with 330 beds. The price per person in a double room is 30 euros, including breakfast and bed linens - quite the bargain! Older individuals and families are also welcome. A hostel card (11 euros) is a must. As an added bonus, Gare du Nord is just a ten-minute walk away. *43, rue Pajol | 19th arr. | tel. 0140 38 87 90 | M 12 Marx Dormoy | www.hifrance.org*

FLATS

The following websites have a large selection of flats and holiday accommodation: *paris.citycosy.com, www.goodmorningparis.fr, www.airbnb.com*

LOFT PARIS (132 B4) *(🕮 K3)*

Five well-equipped large flats as well as a suite situated on a very quiet side street in the middle of Montmartre. Some have a small private courtyard and are furnished with period pieces. Each can accommodate up to six guests – ideal for families, groups or couples. *7, cité Véron | 18th arr. | tel. 06 14 48 47 48 | M 2 Blanche | www. loft-paris.fr*

DISCOVERY TOURS

① PARIS AT A GLANCE

START: ① Fouquet's
END: ⑩ Caveau de la Huchette

Distance:
➡ 27.5 km/17 miles

1 day
Walking time
(without stops)
3 hours

COSTS: Métro/bus tickets 6 euros, Batobus ticket 16 euros, admission for the Musée d'Orsay 11 euros

IMPORTANT TIPS: the nearest Métro station to the start of the tour on the Champs-Elysées is M 1 George V
Reserve a table for dinner at ⑨ Bouillon Racine ahead!
The nearest Métro stations to the last stop on the tour on rue de la Huche are M 4 Saint-Michel or Cité.

Cities have many faces. If you want to get behind the scenes to explore their unique charm and head off the beaten track or find your way to green oases, handpicked restaurants or the best local activities, then these tailored Discovery Tours are just the right thing. Choose the best route for the day and follow in the footsteps of the MARCO POLO authors – well-prepared to navigate your way to all the many highlights that await you along the tour.

With a diameter of approx. 5 km (3.1 miles), the core of the city is smaller than one might expect. You can get a good feel for the metropolis on the water, but the view from the Arc de Triomphe will also help you get your bearings. No visit to Paris would be complete without a stop at the Eiffel Tower and the Louvre, but some of the best art awaits at the Musée d'Orsay. A meal in an Art Nouveau-style restaurant followed by a walk through the lighted streets of Paris cap off the experience.

09:00am Start your day with breakfast on the **Champs-Elysées** → p. 35. One of the most famous of the many street cafés is ❶ **Fouquet's** (daily. | no. 99 | 8th arr. | tel.

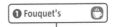
❶ Fouquet's

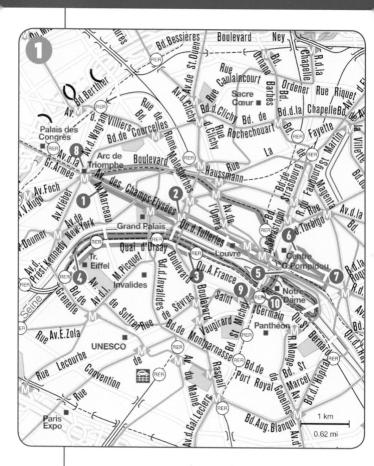

01 40 69 60 50 | Moderate). Photos of film stars with copper plates are a testimonial to the annual César awards. The hustle and bustle along this boulevard with the Arc de Triomphe in the background is a fitting start for a walk through Paris.

10:00am Ride down this impressive avenue on a no. 73 bus, passing by the glass-roofed **Grand Palais and the Petit Palais** → p. 36. As you cross ② **Place de la Concorde** → p. 39 with its stately obelisks and gigantic monumental fountains, you will get a feel for the enormity of this square. **Before the bus turns,** make sure to take a look at the **Jardin des Tuileries** → p. 37, the oldest park in the

② Place de la Concorde

city. It links the square with the Louvre complex. After the bus crosses the Seine, **get off at the stop in front of the ❸ Musée d'Orsay → p. 39.** You will surely be delighted by the tasteful architecture of this converted railway station and the sizeable collection of French Impressionist art that it holds. After a snack at the museum, **take the RER C from the Musée d'Orsay station for three stops to the Eiffel Tower → p. 29.**

`01:00pm` At the foot of this landmark, **on the ❹ Pont d'Iéna bridge, the boats belonging to the Batobus line dock.** Hop aboard and get to know the city from an entirely new perspective on the Seine. During the trip, the boat glides beneath a number of bridges, including the gilded **Pont Alexandre III → p. 40** and the famous **Pont Neuf → p. 53** – bringing you to the heart of the city, the islands on the Seine. The long walls of the former royal seat known as the **Louvre → p. 37,** now the largest museum in the world, stretch along the left-hand side. As the boat circles the islands, you will also be able to admire the Gothic spires of **Notre Dame Cathedral→ p. 51.**

`02:00pm` Disembark at the ❺ **Hôtel de Ville → p. 46** stop. Walk from here along **rue de Rivoli and rue Vieille du Temple** to the nearby bustling district of ❻ **Marais → p. 72.** Check out the numerous small shops such as a branch of the **Uniqlo** chain on rue des Francs-Bourgeois (no. 39) with its inexpensive fashion collections. Then take a break in one of the nostalgic cafés in this quarter. A favourite spot on the impressive former royal square, the **Place des Vosges → p. 48,** is ❼ **Café Hugo** (daily | no. 22 | 4th arr. | tel. 01 42 72 64 04 | Budget–Moderate).

`05:00pm` Head down to the Métro **at the Saint Paul station. Walk down rue de Birague and rue Saint-Antoine to get to the station and then take the M1 to Charles de Gaulle-Étoile.** This underground route will bring you back to the starting point of the tour and just a bit further to the ❽ **Arc de Triomphe → p. 34** and its viewing platform. Twelve avenues converge like a star (étoile) at Place Charles de Gaulle-Étoile, offering the best overview of the layout of the city. By now, you'll surely be ready for diner and you'll hopefully have booked a table at one of the classic Belle-Èpoque restaurants for which Paris is so well-known.

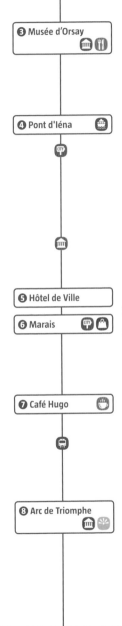

❸ Musée d'Orsay

❹ Pont d'Iéna

❺ Hôtel de Ville

❻ Marais

❼ Café Hugo

❽ Arc de Triomphe

⑨ Bouillon Racine 🍴

08:00pm A particularly good address is **⑨ Bouillon Racine** → p. 66 in the old intellectual neighbourhood of Saint-Germain-des-Prés → p. 82. For the fastest way to get there, **take the RER A from Charles de Gaulle-Étoile and change trains Châtelet-Les Halles to the RER B and get off at Saint-Michel.** The floral designs so typical of the Art Nouveau style cloak the restaurant whose menu is likewise decorative. Enjoy a leisurely meal before delving into the lively nightlife in this area. End the day in true Parisian style at one of the most authentic jazz clubs in the district, **⑩ Caveau de la Huchette** → p. 89.

⑩ Caveau de la Huchette 🍸🎵

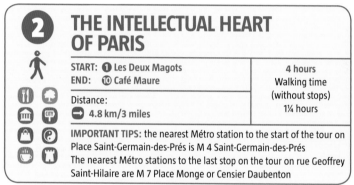

2

THE INTELLECTUAL HEART OF PARIS

START: **❶ Les Deux Magots**	**4 hours**
END: **⑩ Café Maure**	Walking time (without stops)
Distance: ➡ **4.8 km/3 miles**	1¼ hours

IMPORTANT TIPS: the nearest Métro station to the start of the tour on Place Saint-Germain-des-Prés is M 4 Saint-Germain-des-Prés
The nearest Métro stations to the last stop on the tour on rue Geoffrey Saint-Hilaire are M 7 Place Monge or Censier Daubenton

Whereas the right bank *(rive droite)* had long been the place where money was made and spent, the left bank *(rive gauche)* around ★ Saint-Germain-des-Prés and the Quartier Latin was the home of the intellectual scene. In the 1930s and 1950s, much philosophising went on at Café Flore, Les Deux Magots or in the Jardin du Luxembourg. The art academy and university still radiate over this area today, and the free spirit of this tradition lives on. Bask in this inspiration as you walk through the left bank!

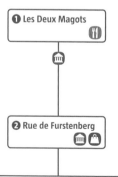
❶ Les Deux Magots 🍴

❷ Rue de Furstenberg 🏛🛍

The patio of **❶ Les Deux Magots** → p. 63 is a bit like a box at the theatre, making it the perfect place to start this tour. Sit back and relax as you watch people stroll past. The church Saint-Germain-des-Prés → p. 53, one of the oldest in Paris, is just opposite. Rue Bonaparte, as well as the other streets in this area, are full of galleries, antique dealers, fabric shops, cafés and restaurants. **Follow rue de l'Abbaye behind the church** to the romantic, tree-lined square on **❷ Rue de Furstenberg**, which was once home to the studio of the artist Eugène Delacroix (no. 6). At no. 7, **INSIDER TIP ▶ La Maison du Chou** sells

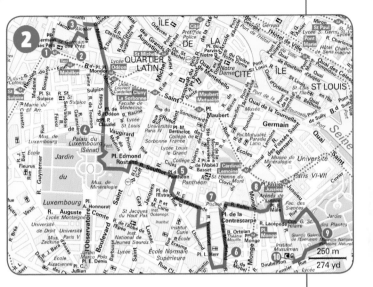

small and delicious cream puffs that make for a perfect little gift. **Then turn right down rue Jacob, which leads to the lively rue de Seine.** Stop for coffee on the patio of the ever-popular ❸ **La Palette → p. 63**. **Continue along rue Jacques Callot, then turn right up rue Mazarine, and head over Boulevard Saint-Germain to rue de l'Odéon.** Walk past the neoclassical Théâtre de l'Odéon until you come to the ❹ **Jardin du Luxembourg → p. 50**, one of the most popular parks in Paris. Take in the Palais du Luxembourg, modelled after the Florentine Palazzo Pitti, as you sit on the edge of the pond or the shaded **Fontaine de Médicis**.

Across from the main entrance, on the other side of the lively Boulevard Saint-Michel with its street cafés, **follow rue Soufflot up to the domed ❺ Panthéon → p. 52**, a mausoleum in which many French luminaries are buried. The narrow lanes that wind up the Montagne Sainte-Geneviève are part of one of the oldest neighbourhoods in Paris.

Walk along rue Malebranche, rue des Fossés Saint-Jacques, which runs through the trench around a medieval city wall, and – after crossing the Place de l'Estrapade with its trees, benches and a fountain – **rue**

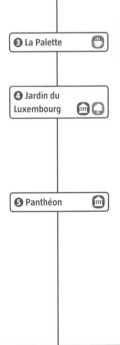

❸ La Palette

❹ Jardin du Luxembourg

❺ Panthéon

Fresh seafood of all kinds at a fishmonger's on rue Mouffetard

de l'Estrapade. These streets exude a tranquillity reminiscent of a provincial town. Thanks to the nearby Sorbonne university and some of the most elite schools in the country, this area is an important centre of intellectual life in the city. **Stroll down rue Laromiguière, rue Amyot and rue Tournefort to rue Lohmond and then turn left into the narrow Passage des Postes,** which is noticeably livelier.

A colourful market with many excellent grocers is situated on the lower end of the very old, yet always bustling **6 Rue Mouffetard → p. 53**. The upper end of the "Mouff" definitely caters more to tourists. But, the food stall **Au p'tit Grec** at no. 66 sells the moistest crêpes in Paris. Eat your crêpe at the upper end of street on **7 Place de la Contrescarpe**, where street musicians and free massages ensure for a moment of relaxation.

From rue du Cardinal Lemoine (Ernest Hemingway once lived at no. 74), **walk down rue Rollin** with its old, crooked houses. **Go down the steps and across rue Monge** to the **8 Arènes de Lutèce**, a Roman amphitheatre, on

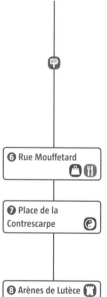

6 Rue Mouffetard

7 Place de la Contrescarpe

8 Arènes de Lutèce

the left-hand side, which was first excavated in the 19th century. Today it is a popular haunt among teenagers. **Head right down rue Linné** (which turns into rue Geoffroy Saint-Hilaire) and go past the Muséum National d'Histoire Naturelle → p. 119 to the **⑨ Jardin des Plantes** → p. 119 with its gardens and greenhouses. **Continue along rue Buffon and rue Daubenton to the Mosquée de Paris**. Delve into an Arabian world with mint tea and sweet honey pastries in the tea room at **⑩ Café Maure** *(daily | rue Geoffroy St-Hilaire 39 | 5th arr. | tel. 0143313820 | www.la-mosquee.com | Budget)* within this wonderfully beautiful mosque.

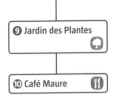

⑨ Jardin des Plantes

⑩ Café Maure

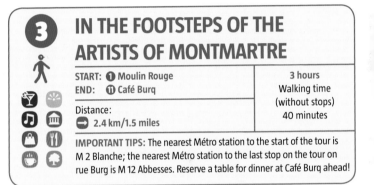

③ IN THE FOOTSTEPS OF THE ARTISTS OF MONTMARTRE

START: ❶ Moulin Rouge **END:** ⑪ Café Burq	3 hours Walking time (without stops) 40 minutes
Distance: ➡ 2.4 km/1.5 miles	

IMPORTANT TIPS: The nearest Métro station to the start of the tour is M 2 Blanche; the nearest Métro station to the last stop on the tour on rue Burg is M 12 Abbesses. Reserve a table for dinner at Café Burq ahead!

★ Montmartre is known as the cradle of modern art. Artists from all over Europe migrated to what was then just a small village on this hill at the turn of the 20th century. As you walk through this district today, you can easily imagine how simple artists, whose works often now hang in the great museums of Paris, went about their daily lives.

The sex trade flourishes around the Métro station Blanche near the **❶ Moulin Rouge** → p. 90, which is still a favourite tourist attraction. Leave this slightly shabby area behind and **walk up the hill via rue Lépic.** Scenes from the cult film Amélie were shot at the **Café des 2 Moulins** at no. 15. Pop in the tiny, old-fashioned bakery across the street at no. 26, **❷ INSIDER TIP Les Petits Mitrons**, whose window display is full of tasty looking tarts. Take in the village-like atmosphere **as you continue along rue Abesses, rue Durantin and up rue Tholozé. When you come to the top of rue Lépic,** enjoy the breathtaking view of the golden dome of the Panthéon → p. 52, which shines

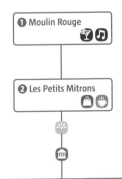

❶ Moulin Rouge

❷ Les Petits Mitrons

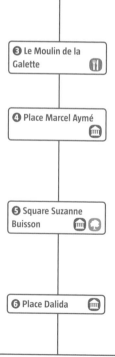

Caulaincourt

above the sea of houses. The garden of the Moulin de la Galette now lies at your feet. The grounds between the two mills, which can still be toured from the outside, were converted into a popular dance hall in the 19th century. Thanks to Auguste Renoir's Impressionist painting of the same name, these gardens are famous around the world. They are now home to the restaurant ❸ **Le Moulin de la Galette** (daily | 83, rue Lepic | tel. 01 46 06 84 77 | www.le moulindelagalette.fr | *Moderate*), which is a great place to take your first break.

❸ Le Moulin de la Galette 🍽

❹ Place Marcel Aymé 🏛

Afterwards, head to ❹ **Place Marcel Aymé**. Look out for the quizzical bronze figure emerging from a wall. The statue depicts the main character of the novella *Le Passe-muraille (The Man Who Walked through Walls)* and is a tribute to the writer Marcel Aymé who once lived on this square. **Follow Avenue Junot and then turn right at the end of rue Simon Dereure** to get to the little park at ❺ **Square Suzanne Buisson**. Sit down and stretch out your legs on one of the benches and admire the **Statue des Saint Denis**. St Denis is said to have walked the same route that you have been following up to now with his head in his hands.

❺ Square Suzanne Buisson 🏛 🌳

❻ Place Dalida 🏛

Return to the entrance and then go up the steps to the right along a small idyllic path to ❻ **Place Dalida**. The statue of the Egyptian-Italian singer (1933–87) looks up rue de l'Abreuvoir, which winds up the hill lined by small, crooked houses in a picture-perfect setting. **At the end of the street and down to the left on rue des Saules**, there is a surprising little ❼ **vineyard**. The grape harvest in October is celebrated with a festival every year, the Fête des Vendanges → p. 121. A few yards further below, the famous cabaret Au Lapin Agile → p. 89 was once owned by the *chanson* singer Aristide Bruant who supported many then poor and unknown musicians at the time.

Rue Saint-Vincent will bring you closer to the back side of the gleaming white, almost Byzantine style basilica of ❽ **Sacré-Cœur** → p. 57. Enjoy the view of Paris from the steps on the front side of the church. The narrow lanes around the church filled with souvenir shops and especially the ❾ **Place du Tertre** → p. 57 are always full of tourists and many rather pushy portrait artists who will try to convince you to have your portrait drawn.

Walk down Rue Norvins until you come to rue Gabrielle (Pablo Picasso had his first studio in no. 49), **and then take rue Ravignan to the tree-lined Place Émile Goudeau.** In a studio within the house named ❿ **Bateau-Lavoir**, Picasso's famous cubist painting *Les Demoiselles d'Avignon* came to life. A bit further down, several lovely restaurants will tempt you to end this tour with a good meal, such as the casual bistro ⑪ **Café Burq** *(closed Sun/Mon | rue Burq 6 | 18th arr. | tel. 01 42 52 81 27 | Moderate).*

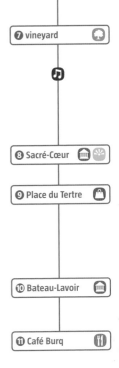

❼ vineyard

❽ Sacré-Cœur

❾ Place du Tertre

❿ Bateau-Lavoir

⑪ Café Burq

With street cafés and portrait painters, Place du Tertre has an almost provincial flair

THE ISLANDS ON THE SEINE AND MARAIS

4

START: ❶ Musée de Cluny
END: ⓮ Musée Picasso

Distance:
➡ 4 km/2.5 miles

| 6 hours |
| Walking time |
| (without stops) |
| 1 hour |

COSTS: admission to Musée Picasso: 11 euros

IMPORTANT TIPS: the nearest Métro station to the start of the tour on Place Paul Painlevé is M 10 Cluny-La Sorbonne
Hôtel de Sens: temporary exhibitions in the Bibliothèque Forney (equipment.paris.fr/bibliotheque-forney-18)
The nearest Métro station to the last stop on the tour on rue de Thorigny is M8 Chemin Vert

The islands Ile de la Cité and Ile Saint-Louis are the heart of the metropolis, especially given that the first seeds of the city were sown upon them. The Marais district shines with the glory of the aristocratic palaces *(hôtel particulier)* that were build around the royal square, Place des Vosges, at the beginning of the 17th century. Many Parisians say that this Renaissance-style square in this quite stylish part of town is the most beautiful in the whole city.

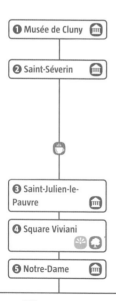

❶ Musée de Cluny

❷ Saint-Séverin

❸ Saint-Julien-le-Pauvre

❹ Square Viviani

❺ Notre-Dame

The small park in the shadows of the Roman spas around the ❶ **Musée de Cluny** → p. 51 is the perfect place to start off on the day's tour. A labyrinth of medieval streets begins **on the other side of Boulevard Saint-Germain** around the flamboyant Gothic-style church of ❷ **Saint-Séverin**. The distinguishing features of the church include its five-aisled nave and the double row of columns around the apse. The ribbed vaulted ceiling resembles plant stalks with colourful modern glass windows peeking through. The neighbourhood is full of inviting little cafés such as **La Fourmi Ailée** → p. 68, where you'll be tempted to linger, but also many restaurants that vie for tourist business.

Just a short walk down rue Saint-Séverin will bring you to the small, stocky church of ❸ **Saint-Julien-le-Pauvre**, the oldest church in the city dating back to the 12th century. From the adjacent park at ❹ **Square Viviani**, you can enjoy the view of the Seine as well as the boxes of Les Bouquinistes → p. 74 and ❺ **Notre Dame Cathedral**

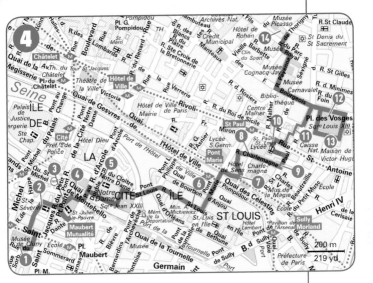

→ p. 51 in peace and quiet. You simply must go inside the cathedral! A lovely garden brings life to the eastern side of the church. Look for the **little bridge that connects the Île de la Cité → p. 48** with the **Île Saint-Louis**. Both islands, as the oldest parts of the city, are the real heart of Paris. Street artists almost always ply their trade on the strip connecting the two. Take some time to window shop on rue Saint-Louis-en-l'Île with its lovely little shops and the best ice cream in the city at **⑥ Amorino → p. 75.**

The Pont Marie bridge will lead you directly into the Marais quarter. Directly to the right, at the corner of rue de l'Hôtel de Ville and rue du Figuier, the fortress-like late Gothic **⑦ Hôtel de Sens** will surely catch your eye. This former second residence of the powerful bishops of the city of Sens now houses the art library INSIDER TIP **Bibliothèque Forney. At the end of rue du Figuier, you will stumble upon rue Charlemagne** and the charming little patio restaurant **⑧ Chez Mademoiselle** (daily | rue Charlemagne 16 | 4th arr. | tel. 0142721416 | Budget–Moderate).

After a bite to eat, **continue along rue Charlemagne,** past the ruins of a tower and the old city walls dating back to the 13th century. Spend some time browsing through

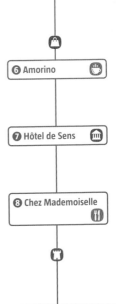

⑥ Amorino

⑦ Hôtel de Sens

⑧ Chez Mademoiselle

⑨ Village Saint-Paul 🛍

⑩ Saint-Paul 🏛

⑪ Place du Marché Sainte-Catherine ☕

⑫ Place des Vosges 🚶

⑬ Maison Victor Hugo 🏛

⑭ Musée Picasso 🏛 🍴

the courtyard labyrinth of **⑨ Village Saint-Paul → p. 74**, which is home to approx. 60 antiques dealers selling furniture, artworks, tableware, lamps and jewellery.

Continue left up rue Saint-Paul to the Passage Saint-Paul, which leads through a side entrance into the three-storey Baroque church of **⑩ Saint-Paul** with its large cupola. The traffic buzzes on rue Saint-Antoine in front of the main entrance. **Walk a bit further towards the Bastille and turn left on rue Caron** to get to the romantic **⑪ Place du Marché Sainte-Catherine → p. 48** with its sycamore trees and cafés. Take a moment to catch your breath before **heading over rue de Turenne to the right onto the lively rue des Francs-Bourgeois,** which is lined by lovely aristocratic palaces. From here, it is just a short walk to the noble **⑫ Place des Vosges → p. 48**, one of the loveliest squares in the city. Take a walk around it, and, if you want, have a look at the former flat (marked by the flag on the southeastern corner of the square) of the French national poet at **⑬ Maison Victor Hugo → p. 46**. **Cross back over the square to rue des Francs-Bourgeois, go right on rue Payenne and go via rue du Parc Royal to turn down rue de Thorigny.** The most extensive Picasso collection in the world awaits at the **⑭ Musée Picasso → p. 47** in Hôtel Salé. End the day in style at the **Café sur le toit** (*Tue–Sun 11:30am–6pm, 3rd Fri in the month until 9pm | tel. 01 44 61 79 19 | Budget*).

Victor Hugo began work on his masterpiece *Les Misérables* in this room

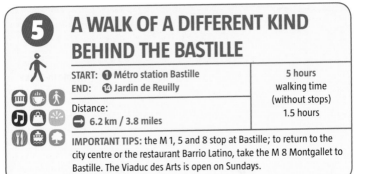

⑤ A WALK OF A DIFFERENT KIND BEHIND THE BASTILLE

START: ❶ Métro station Bastille	5 hours
END: ⑭ Jardin de Reuilly	walking time (without stops)
Distance: ➡ 6.2 km / 3.8 miles	1.5 hours

IMPORTANT TIPS: the M 1, 5 and 8 stop at Bastille; to return to the city centre or the restaurant Barrio Latino, take the M 8 Montgallet to Bastille. The Viaduc des Arts is open on Sundays.

In the 19th century, craftsmen ruled over the eastern part of the city behind the Bastille. Nowadays, many of the former workshops *(cours)* have been turned into nostalgic, modern lofts popular among the young and creative crowd. The old train tracks (4.5km / 2.8 miles) running from the east have been transformed into a walking path, and artisans have set up shop in the old aqueduct.

The ❶ **Métro station Bastille** marks the starting point for this tour to the east of the city centre. Nothing remains of the Bastille, the state prison that was stormed in 1789 at the outbreak of the French Revolution. Today, the outline of the former structure is traced in stones different from the rest of the pavement on Place de la Bastille where it intersects with Boulevard Henri IV. Go directly to the shining silver Opéra Bastille → p. 47 and leave this huge, traffic-filled square in the **direction of rue du Faubourg Saint-Antoine.** If you keep a lookout for hidden entrances, you will stumble upon some of the old craftsmen's workshops.

Right at the start of rue de la Roquette (no. 2), you will come upon the quiet ❷ **Passage du Cheval Blanc**, which is divided into courtyards named after the first six months of the year. **Turn right onto Cité Parchappe to return to rue du Faubourg Saint-Antoine,** which is lined by a string of idyllic courtyards, such as the **Cour Saint-Louis** or the **Cour Vigues.**

Across from the restaurant ❸ **Barrio Latino** → p. 84, where you should make reservations for the evening, **turn left onto rue de Charonne,** a lively shopping street. At no. 41, treat yourself to a *café crème* on the

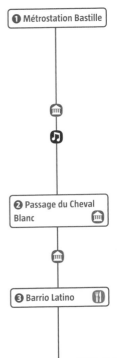

❶ Métrostation Bastille

❷ Passage du Cheval Blanc

❸ Barrio Latino

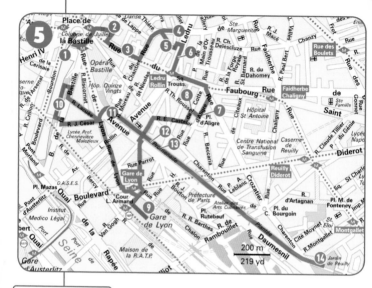

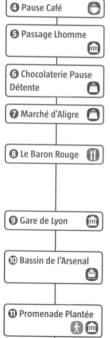

④ Pause Café	☕
⑤ Passage Lhomme	🏛
⑥ Chocolaterie Pause Détente	🏬
⑦ Marché d'Aligre	🏬
⑧ Le Baron Rouge	🍴
⑨ Gare de Lyon	🏛
⑩ Bassin de l'Arsenal	⚓
⑪ Promenade Plantée	🚶🏛

patio of the trendy ④ **Pause Café** → p. 69. Afterwards, cross through the lushly landscaped, picturesque ⑤ **Passage Lhomme** until it emerges onto Avenue Ledru-Rollin. Stop at no. 98 and select some chocolates from ⑥ **Chocolaterie Pause Détente** *(closed Mon)* to eat as you walk on. **Then cross rue Crozatier to rue d'Aligre, which will take you directly to Place d'Aligre.** At the 200-year old, still very authentic market hall of ⑦ INSIDER TIP **Marché d'Aligre** *(closed Mon | www.marchedaligre.free. fr)*, you will find no end of delicious cheeses, hams, sausages and cold cuts. A good glass of wine and a few oysters at ⑧ **Le Baron Rouge** → p. 71 are just right for a little break.

With this fine taste lingering in your mouth, **follow rue Emilio Castelar and then rue Traversière to get to** ⑨ **Gare de Lyon**, the loveliest railway station in the city and home to the legendary restaurant **Le Train Bleu** → p. 65. Then take **rue de Lyon and rue Jules César** to the picture-perfect harbour ⑩ **Bassin de l'Arsenal**. The port has an almost maritime flair thanks to the many yachts that lay anchor here. **Go back via rue Lacuée to Avenue Daumnesnil,** which will bring you to this tour's major highlight, namely the ⑪ **Promenade Plantée** (aka: Coulée Verte). These former train tracks now surrounded by plenty of vegetation lead 4.5 km (2.8 miles) from the Bastille to the forest of Vincennes.

For the first 1.5 km (1 mile), the red brick arches of the former railway viaduct have been glassed in to create studio space for all kinds of artisans and craftsmen. Whilst products are made and sold in the shops below, you can walk along the planted roof. **There are plenty of stairs that will take you up the 9 m (30 ft) to the top.** In the 55 studio shops within the ⑫ **Viaduc des Arts** → p. 81, only the finest materials are used. Fashion designers, goldsmiths, picture restorers, glass-blowers and many shops selling art as opposed to crafts are housed in this innovative space. For something a bit different, check out the jewellery designer **Tzuri Gueta** (no. 1) who, among other things, creates silicon objects that resemble underwater plants. Interesting jewellery is also created at **Cécile et Jeanne** (no. 49) If you have deeper pockets, you can buy your own unique made-to-order handbag at **Serge Amoruso** (no. 37) or have an umbrella designed and made just for you at **Heurtault** (no. 85). If all this shopping has made you hungry, the best and most convenient place to go is the ⑬ **Viaduc Café** (daily | no. 41 | tel. 01 44 74 70 70 | www.leviaduc-cafe. com | Budget).

Once you're duly refreshed, climb up to the "roof" of the viaduct and admire the urban walking trail. Between the rose bushes, lavender and babbling water, you can appreciate the extraordinary view of the surrounding metropolitan area. **As you continue to the east**, you will come to the small park ⑭ **Jardin de Reuilly**, which is spanned by a footbridge and a favourite place among the locals in the neighbourhood during the summer. Take time to relax for a bit in the park before you head back.

| ⑫ Viaduc des Arts | 🛍 |
| ⑬ Viaduc Café | 🍴 |
| 🚶 |
| ⑭ Jardin de Reuilly | 🪴 |

Ateliers and shops beneath the old vaults of the Viaduc des Arts

TRAVEL WITH KIDS

AQUABOULEVARD (156 B5) (⌖ D12)
One of the largest water parks in Europe, featuring pools with waterfalls and a number of fun waterslides under its glass roof. *Mon–Thu 9am–11pm, Fri 9am–midnight, Sat 8am–midnight | admission 20 euros, April–Sept 29 euros, children 3–11 yr. 19 euros | Porte de Sèvres | 4, rue Louis Armand | 15th arr. | M 8 Balard | www.parcs-aquatiques.com*

CANAL SAINT-MARTIN
Impressive, three-hour canal trip between the Musée d'Orsay (146 A4) (⌖ J7) and the Parc de la Villette (143 E2) (⌖ Q2) through locks, bridges and tunnels. *Mar–Nov daily | departure: 9:30am from the Quai Anatole France or 2:30pm from Parc de la Villette | fare 19 euros, children 16 euros | tel. 01 42 40 96 97 | www.pariscanal.com*

CIRQUE D'HIVER (148 B4) (⌖ O7)
The magnificent circus venue which has existed for over 150 years is regarded as one of the most beautiful in the world. The Bouglione family provides the best in circus tradition from September to March. *Fri 8:30pm, Sat/Sun 2pm, 5:15pm, 8:30pm | admission 27–62 euros | 110, rue Amelot | 11th arr. | M 8 Filles du Calvaire | www.cirquedhiver.com*

CITÉ DES SCIENCES ET DE L'INDUSTRIE ★ (143 E2) (⌖ Q1–2)
A futuristic science museum where visitors can pretend to be researchers with a submarine, flight simulator and planetarium. The giant silver ball *La Géode* provides a 360-degree big screen presentation on scientific topics every hour. *Tue–Sat 10am–6pm, Sun 10am–7pm | prices structured according to selection of attractions starting at 9 euros; free admission for children under 7 yr. | 30, av. Cortenin Cariiou | 19th arr. | M 7 Porte de la Villette | www.cite-sciences.f*

DISNEYLAND PARIS (0) (⌖ 0)
Every year up to 12 Million visitors walk through the gates of Walt Disney's fairytale dreamland, making it one of Europe's most important tourist attractions. *Changing opening hours, posted daily on the website | day pass from 45 euros, children from 39 euros | info on current special attractions can be found on the website | 40 km (25mi) east of Paris | RER A Marne-de-la Vallée or Val d'Europe | www.disneylandparis.fr*

JARDIN D'ACCLIMATATION (136–137 B–E6) (⌖ B4–5)
In this elegant area in the Bois de Boulogne, this garden exudes the charm of

**Fun for kids of all ages:
A trip to Paris can be a memorable
experience for children**

the 19th century with its unusual play-ground areas, carousels, animals and water features. *Daily 10am–7pm | admission 3 euros | M 1 Les Sablons | www.jardindacclimatation.fr*

JARDIN DES PLANTES
(153 F2–3) (𝄞 N10)
Something to suit every age group: at the Jardin des Plantes with its *horticultural teaching garden (daily 7:30am–7pm)* there is also the INSIDER TIP *Ménagerie (daily 9am–6pm | admission 13 euros, children 9 euros, free under 4 yr.)*, a well laid out zoo for smaller children with reptiles, monkeys, wildcats and old trees. On the side of the park opposite the zoo, older children can explore the ★ *Musée National d'Histoire Naturelle (daily 10am–6pm | admission 7 euros, free under 26 yr.)*. In the entrance hall there is a fascinating caravan of stuffed life-size animals. You can also check out the complexes for *palaeontology* (with huge dinosaur bones) and *mineralogy (Palaeontology and mineralogy: daily 10am–5pm |*

admission 7 euros each, free under 26 yr.). The ● greenhouses, *Les Grandes Serres (summer: Wed–Mon 10am–6pm, Sun until 6:30pm; winter: 10am–5pm | admission 6 euros, children 4 euros (free under 4 yr.)*, with their rain forest-like vegetation are also fantastic. *57, rue Cuvier | 5th arr. | M 5, 10 Gare d'Austerlitz |RER C | www.mnhn.fr | www.jardindesplantes.net*

PARC ASTÉRIX (0) (𝄞 0)
An excellent French alternative to Disneyland, if not a bit smaller. Asterix and his friends captivate visitors to the theme park with all sorts of fun activities and a replica of the small village of the indomitable Gauls. *April–Aug Mon–Fri 10am–6pm, Sat/Sun 9:30am–7pm (May/June Tue and Thu partly closed), Sept/Oct Wed, Sat, Sun 10am–6pm | admission 46 euros, children (3–11 yr.) 37 euros | 60-Plailly (30 km (18½mi) north of Paris) | by bus: from the Louvre coach park (M 1, 7 Palais Royal-Louvre) departure: 9am (22 euros) | by car: motorway A 1, exit: Parc Astérix | www.parcasterix.fr*

FESTIVALS & EVENTS

EVENTS

FEBRUARY

Chinese New Year: colourful procession around the Place d'Italie (dates vary)

MARCH–APRIL

Foire à la Brocante et au Jambon: large antique trade fair (additional date in October). *RER A Chatou-Croissy*

Banlieues Bleues: first-rate jazz festival in Saint-Denis and other suburbs. *www.banlieuesbleues.org*

APRIL

Paris Marathon: begins at 9am on the Champs-Elysées (last Sunday of the month)

Printemps des Musées: on one Sunday between March and May during the spring museum festival, all museums are free of charge.

MAY–JUNE

Festival de Saint-Denis: the classical music festival starts at the end of May and continues for four weeks. *www.festival-saint-denis.fr*

JUNE

INSIDER TIP *Concours International des Roses:* classical concerts amidst blooming roses in Parc de Bagatelle in the Bois de Boulogne

⭐ *Fête de la Musique:* free concerts on nearly every street corner in the city all night long (21/22 June).

Gay Parade: a gay and lesbian procession from the Porte Dorée to the Bastille (fourth Saturday)

JUNE–JULY

INSIDER TIP *Paris Jazz Festival:* free concerts with international jazz greats in the Parc Floral des Bois de Vincennes every weekend. *www.parisjazzfestival.fr*

JULY

Bastille Day: large military parade on the Champs-Elysées and fireworks on the Place du Trocadéro, folk festivals with dancing on public squares the night before (14 July)

Tour de France: final stage on the Champs-Elysées (last or second to last Sunday)

JULY–AUGUST

● INSIDER TIP *Paris-Plages:* various beach activities for five weeks beginning in mid-July. *www.paris-plages.fr*

The metropolis offers something for everyone: music, theatre, cinema, sport, cultural events and colourful parades

Quartier d'Eté: many free concerts in parks and on small squares (from mid-July)
Open-air Cinema: free drive-in theatre at Parc de la Villette (from mid-July)

AUGUST
Rock en Seine: well-known rock music greats perform for three days in the Parc de Saint-Cloud. *www.rockenseine.com*

SEPTEMBER
Journée du Patrimoine: free admission to public buildings otherwise closed to the general public (third weekend)

SEPTEMBER–DECEMBER
⭐ *Festival d'Automne:* autumn festival with spectacular contemporary theatre, music and dance performances. *www. festival-automne.com*

OCTOBER
Fête des Vendanges: grape harvest on Montmartre (first Saturday)

Fiac: extensive contemporary art fair (five days of the month)
INSIDER TIP *Nuit Blanche:* music and art happenings in unusual places (usually the first Saturday). *www.paris.fr*

NATIONAL HOLIDAYS

1 Jan	New Year's Day
28 March 2016, 17 April 2017	
	Easter Monday
1 May	Labour Day
8 May	Victory Day
5 May 2016, 25 May 2017	
	Ascension Day
14 July	Bastille Day
15 Aug	Assumption of Mary
1 Nov	All Saints' Day
11 Nov	Armistice Day
25 Dec	Christmas

LINKS, BLOGS, APPS & MORE

LINKS & BLOGS

en.parisinfo.com Official website for Paris supplying extensive information on a variety of current events. Also helpful in finding accommodation

en.visitparisregion.com Website for Paris and the surrounding region, with events calendar, suggested walks and much more

www.facebook.com/paristourisme Always the latest news on what is happening in Paris

www.paris-26-gigapixels.com Inspiring interactive page which uses the Google Earth principle to navigate through Paris and to simultaneously obtain information about the most important attractions

www.mylittleparis.com Lifestyle tips – restaurants, beauty & fashion, special sales and more

www.myparisianlife.com Stylish blog by a New York expat – eating, drinking, shopping, beauty, activities with kids and much more, sorted by arrondissement, if you want

www.easyfashion.blogspot.com Fred Vielcanet takes pictures of stylish people in the streets of Paris. Inspiring.

www.parisforums.com Comprehensive forum with themes such as accommodation, culture, buying and selling, sports, health, etc.

www.expat-blog.com/en/natio nalities/british/in/europe/france/ paris Informative forum for expats living in Paris. Includes photos and the opportunity to join in and meet fellow expats

Regardless of whether you are still preparing your trip or already in Paris: these addresses will provide you with more information, videos and networks to make your holiday even more enjoyable

www.youtube.com/watch?v=RfDv5TTJ3Bc A quick-paced visit to Paris: a tourist whizzes through the city in 24 hours in fast-forward camera motion

www.youtube.com/watch?v=sWTLdmBoy_k A short film featuring the popular singer ZAZ and a street band in Montmartre

https://www.youtube.com/watch?v=blw8zJt-ScO Paris as it was in the 1920s — nostalgic footage from boulevards and cafés

https://www.youtube.com/watch?v=-64kHmCJGMA 3 D animation of the city of Paris through the ages — watch, for example, the construction of the Eiffel Tower

Musée du Louvre The most important 100 pictures of about 35,000 are interactively shown in this iPhone app

Le Grand Palais Popular iPhone-app of the monuments architecture with comments from the master himself — Karl Lagerfeld

Fotopedia Paris App for iOS devices. Over 4,000 photographs of Paris with accompanying descriptions

www.spottedbylocals.com/paris The community "Spotted by Locals" posts tips about the best places in the city

TRAVEL TIPS

ARRIVAL

All roads lead to the ring road Boulevard Périphérique. In Paris it is advisable to leave your car parked at the hotel; nearly all motorways are subject to toll charges. Speed limit: 130 km/h (80 mph).

You can travel between London and Paris by coach for as little as 21 euros one way. Check out the National Express connections between London and Paris (including DIsneyland Paris) at www.eurolines.co.uk.

The high-speed train, TGV (Eurostar) arrives at the Gare du Nord from London. The railway station has a connection to the Métro network and the RER B can also be accessed from the Gare du Nord. If you book early enough, you can travel from London to Paris return from 88 euros.

RESPONSIBLE TRAVEL

It doesn't take a lot to be environmentally friendly whilst travelling. Don't just think about your carbon footprint whilst flying to and from your holiday destination but also about how you can protect nature and culture abroad. As a tourist it is especially important to respect nature, look out for local products, cycle instead of driving, save water and much more. If you would like to find out more about eco-tourism please visit: *www.ecotourism.org*

Due to stiff competition, you can often get a cheap flight to Paris by booking in advance, and even bargains can be found at short notice. Return flights are often available through easyjet from 99 euros. Compare airfares on the Internet under *www.skyscanner. net*.

Scheduled flights out of the UK land either at Charles-de-Gaulle (CDG) airport north of Paris, or at Orly to the south of the city.

There is a free shuttle service to the RER station from Terminal 1 (CDG). Air France flies out of Terminal 2. Trains operate from the RER and TGV stations to the inner city (Châtelet-Les Halles) between 4:56am and 11:55pm, for 9.75 euros.

Air France buses run every 20 minutes between 6am and 11pm from both terminals to the Étoile and Porte Maillot and back to the airport for 16.20 euros each way, and to Gare de Lyon as well as Gare Montparnasse from 6am–9pm every 30 minutes (and until 9:30pm in the opposite direction), for 16.50 euros. *lescarsairfrance.com*

The Roissy bus run by RATP travels from CDG–Opéra (rue Scribe) between 5:45am and 11pm (6am–11pm in the opposite direction) every 15–20 minutes, for 11.60 euros.

From Orly, direct RATP buses operate every 15–20 minutes to the RER station Denfert-Rochereau (6am–11:20pm; 5:35am–11:05pm in the opposite direction). Travel time is approx. 30 minutes, for 8.50 euros. You can also take the Orlyval from Orly (6am–11pm) to the Antony station and transfer to the RER B

From arrival to weather

Holiday from start to finish: the most important addresses and information for your Paris trip

from there. Total travel time (including transfer) to and from the inner city is approx. 40 minutes, for 12.85 euros (RER plus Orlyval).

Taxis: a trip to the inner city costs between 50 and 55 euros.

BIKE RENTALS

With over 1,800 stations city-wide, the Velib bike rental system *(www.velib.fr)* is incredibly popular. All you need is a credit card to pay the 1.70 euro basic fee per day (the first 30 minutes is free) plus a usage fee for each half hour thereafter. The velib stations are marked on most city maps. The Velib app is also useful because it notes at which stations bikes are available.

CUSTOMS

Within the European Union the following quality and quantity limits apply for personal consumption: 800 cigarettes, 1 kg tobacco, 10 l spirits. For wine there's no benchmark.

DRIVING IN PARIS

The same traffic regulations apply here as elsewhere in Europe. Parisians tend to speed, but do not insist of having the right of way. Parking in the wrong spot can be expensive: you run the risk of having your wheels clamped (to unlock them, contact the nearest police station) or even towed away. The blood-alcohol limit is 0.5 mg/ml. Car and motorbike riders have to pay a fine of 11 euros if they do not carry with them the obligatory breathalizer

(éthylotest). You can purchase these disposable units for 1 euro in drugstores, service areas, petrol stations and supermarkets. Petrol is about as costly as in other large European cities, and you're best advised to fill up at the more inexpensive garages at major supermarkets.

BUDGETING

Coffee	from 2.50 euros *for an espresso*
Snack	from 4.20 euros *for a ham sandwich*
Wine	from 4.50 euros *for a glass of table wine*
Croissant	1.50 euros
Souvenir	13.60 euros *for 6 macarons from Ladurée*
Taxi	8.50 euros *for a short trip approx. 3km*

EMBASSIES & CONSULATES

BRITISH EMBASSY
35, rue du Faubourg St Honoré | 75383 Paris Cedex 08 | tel. 01 44 51 31 00 | www.gov.uk/government/world/france

EMBASSY OF THE UNITED STATES
2, avenue Gabriel | 75382 Paris Cedex 08 | tel. 01 43 12 22 22 | france.usembassy.gov

EMBASSY OF CANADA
35, avenue Montaigne | 75008 Paris | tel. 01 44 43 29 00 | www.france.gc.ca

EMERGENCY SERVICES

– Ambulance (Samu): dial 15
– Police: dial 17
– Fire department, First Aid: dial 18
– Medical emergencies (SOS Médecins): tel. 01 47 07 77 77
– Dental emergencies: tel. 01 43 37 51 00

GUIDED TOURS

BATOBUS
Every 20–25 minutes a ferry crosses the Seine between the Eiffel Tower and Jardin des Plantes. You can board or disembark the boat at any of the total of eight stops. *April–Aug 10am–9:30pm, Sept–March 10am–7pm | 1-day ticket 16 euros | www.batobus.com*

LES CARS ROUGES
The red double decker buses operate every 10–20 minutes from 9:30am to 6pm (last departure from Trocadéro). You can board the bus at any stop. The route includes all important sightseeing attractions. A two-day ticket is 31 euros, 10 percent cheaper if booked online. *Tel. 01 53 95 39 53 | www.carsrouges.com*

PARIS L'OPEN TOUR
The open double decker buses operate on three different routes that include 30 stops. You can board or disembark at any stop. *April–Oct daily 9am–8pm, Nov–March daily 9am–6pm | 1-day ticket 32 euros, for two days 36 euros | main departure stop: 13, rue Auber | 9th arr. | M 3, 9 Havre-Caumartin | RER A Auber | tel. 01 42 66 56 56 | www.parislopentour.com*

DISCOVERWALKS
http://www.discoverwalks.com/paris-walking-tours/

INFORMATION BEFORE YOU TRAVEL

THE FRENCH TOURIST BOARD
– Atout France | Lincoln House | 300 High Holborn | WC1V 7JH London | info.uk@france.fr | www.france.fr
– Atout France | 825 3rd Avenue | New York, NY 10022 | tel. 212-838-7800 | info.us@france.fr | www.france.fr

INFORMATION IN PARIS

OFFICE DU TOURISME ET DES CONGRÈS DE PARIS
Accommodation service for a small fee (reservations in advance are not possible), tickets, package tours, information. *25, rue des Pyramides | 1st arr. | tel. 08 92 68 30 00 | www.parisinfo.com | M 7, 14 Pyramides, RER A Auber | June–Oct daily 9am–7pm, Nov–May Mon–Sat 10am–7pm, Sun 11am–7pm*

Additional offices: *Gare de Lyon (20, boul. Diderot |12th arr. | Mon–Sat 8am–6pm), Gare du Nord (18, rue de Dunkerque | 10th arr. | daily 8am–6pm), Gare de l'Est (pl. du 11 novembre 1918 |10th arr. | Mon–Sat 7am–8pm), Trocadéro (pl. du Trocadéro | 16th arr.) | daily 11am–7pm), Notre-Dame (6, Parvis de N. D. | 4th arr. | daily 10am–7pm), Bastille (pl. de la Bastille | 11th arr. | daily 11am–7pm), Champs-Elysées (ave. Marigny | 8th arr. | April–Oct daily 9am–7pm), Montmartre (21, pl. du Tertre | 18th arr. | daily 10am–7pm).*

INTERNET & WIFI

Paris wants to become a digital metropolis. Around 400 public squares, parks and buildings such as libraries and the Centre Pompidou offer free WiFi. Signs denote places with WiFi. The service is usually accessible from 7am to 11pm.

An increasing number of cafés, bars, restaurants as well as hotels and youth hostels provide *wifi gratuit.* Some Métro and RER stations are equipped with Internet stations with free access. You can find a list of WiFi hotspots at *www. cafes-wifi.com.*

LOST & FOUND

BUREAU DES OBJETS TROUVÉS
36, rue des Morillons | 15th arr. | tel. 08 21 00 25 25 | M12 Convention | Mon–Thu 8:30am–5pm, Fri 8:30am–4:30pm

MEDICAL SERVICES

EU citizens are entitled to the same health benefits as the French by means of the European Health Insurance Card (EHIC). You can also offset physician expenses through the French social insurance provider, although a full refund is not typically issued. Travel insurance is recommended – also for US citizens.

Chemists *(pharmacies)* are denoted by a green cross and are generally open until 8pm Mon–Sat, or even later. The *Pharmacie Les Champs (Dhery)* is open around the clock (*84, ave. des Champs-Elysées | Galeries des Champs-Elysées | 8th arr. | tel. 01 45 62 02 41 | M1 George V).*

PHONES & MOBILE PHONES

You can obtain telephone cards *(télécartes)* at *café tabacs,* kiosks or at the post office in various denominations. You can receive phone calls in booths marked with bells and telephone numbers (significantly less expensive than a mobile phone).

All Paris numbers (with the exception of special numbers) begin with 01 and have ten digits. The country code for the UK is +44, for the USA +1, and then the area code without a zero. When calling from overseas, +331 must be dialled for Paris phone numbers (leaving out the zero for Paris), and then the eight digit telephone number.

The French word for mobile phone is *portable.* Save on incoming calls by purchasing a French prepaid card, which doesn't add surcharges.

POST

Main post office: *52, rue du Louvre | 1st arr. | M 4 Les Halles | daily, 24 hours.* Cost of sending postcards and letters up to 20 grams within the EU is 80 cents.

PUBLIC TRANSPORT

The Métro, complemented by the underground urban area RER railway system and the local buses, covers nearly every corner of Paris. A free network map is available at all stations and in Offices du Tourisme. If you're changing trains or trams, note that many stations have long passageways and flights of stairs.

Métro and RER operate from 5:30am–12:30am, Fri and Sat until approx. 2am, but buses only from 6:30am–8:30pm. Night buses *(noctilien)* run between 12:30am and 5:30am every hour from Châtelet (1:30am, 2:30am, etc.).

Bus trips can make for an interesting alternative to the Métro because they are a great way to see the city. This is especially the case for bus number 73 (Arc de Triomphe, Champs-Elysées, Place de la Concorde, Musée d'Orsay) and number 21 (Opéra Garnier, Louvre, Palais Royal, St-Michel, Île de la Cité, Jardin du Luxembourg, Rue Mouffetard). Besides, a

INSIDER TIP city tour by bus will only cost you 1.80 euros!

White tickets are valid within the city limits for the Métro, RER, tram and buses. They are valid for two hours on the Métro and RER, with as many transfers as you wish, as long as you remain in the city zones. You must validate your tickets on the bus, Métro and RER and have them ready to show upon request. Tickets can be purchased at tobacco shops marked with the ticket pictogram, in all Métro and RER stations as well as from bus drivers. A single ticket costs 1.80 euros (a night bus can cost 1–3 single tickets, depending on the distance). It is more economical to purchase a book of 10 tickets *(carnet)* for 14.10 euros. Children up to four years of age travel for free.

There are a variety of discounts available to tourists. The day card *Carte Mobilis* costs 7 euros. The two zones in which the ticket can be used cover the inner city. The *Paris Visite* ticket costs 12.30 euros per day and offers additional discounts for Disneyland Paris; main attractions, however, are not included. The all-inclusive ticket *Paris Visite* for 1, 2, 3 or 5 days provides discounts for sightseeing and costs 20 euros for 2 days (valid only within the city).

The *Paris Navigo Decouverte* (21.25 euros, plus 5 euros for the ticket and a passport photo) is ideal for a longer Paris stay. It allows you to travel as often as you wish in zones 1 and 2 on weekdays. You can only purchase these tickets on Mondays at Métro stations or tourist information offices. They can also be purchased via the Internet prior to your holiday. Further information available at *www.ratp.fr*

SEINE EXCURSIONS

Tourist boats – usually glazed and with an upper deck that can be opened –

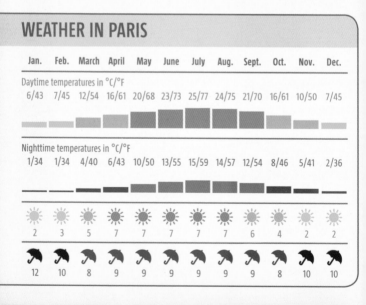

WEATHER IN PARIS

	Jan.	Feb.	March	April	May	June	July	Aug.	Sept.	Oct.	Nov.	Dec.
Daytime temperatures in °C/°F												
	6/43	7/45	12/54	16/61	20/68	23/73	25/77	24/75	21/70	16/61	10/50	7/45
Nighttime temperatures in °C/°F												
	1/34	1/34	4/40	6/43	10/50	13/55	15/59	14/57	12/54	8/46	5/41	2/36
☀	2	3	5	7	7	7	7	7	6	4	2	2
🌂	12	10	8	9	9	9	9	9	9	8	10	10

that travel up and down the Seine are ubiquitous in Paris. The first of these boats known as *bateaux mouches* was launched in 1949, and they have since become very popular as passing the sights on the river is a lovely way to see things. The boats, carrying as many as a hundred passengers, glide under bridges and past imposing palaces, night and day. Dinners on board when the city glows at night are just as popular. Around 50 companies offer excursions, the largest of which is still the pioneer, the *Bateaux Mouches,* which has nine boats and caters to 130,000 diners a year. *Trips during high season: 10am–10:30pm, every 20 min. | departure: Port de la Conférence, Pont de l'Alma (8th arr.) | M9 Alma-Marceau | duration: 70 min. | price: 13.50 euros, 55 euros with lunch, 99–145 euros with dinner.* Other companies are listed under: *www.bateauxparisiens.com*.

TAXIS

Taxis charge a base fee of 6.40 euros and cost between 0.96 and 1.21 euros per km (depending on the time of travel). A taxi ride is more expensive at night, at weekends, with luggage and from railway stations. Always request a receipt *(reçu)*. If you leave something in the taxi, contact the *Préfecture de Police, Service des Taxis (rue des Morillons | 15th arr. | tel. 01 55 76 20 00 | M12 Convention)*.

– *General tel. 01 45 30 30 30*
– *Taxi G7: tel. 01 47 39 47 39*
– *Taxis Bleus: tel. 08 91 70 10 10*
– *Aéro Taxi: tel. 01 47 39 01 47*

TICKET SALES

The Office du Tourisme helps obtain tickets. A ticket service is available at *www.ticketnet.fr* as well as:

– *Fnac: Forum des Halles | 1, rue Pierre Lescot | 1st arr. | tel. 08 92 68 36 22 | M/ RER Châtelet-Les Halles* and *74, ave. des Champs-Elysées | 8th arr. | tel. 01 53 53 64 64 | www.fnac.com | M 1 George V.*

WHAT'S ON

Pariscope (0.50 euros), *L'Officiel du Spectacle* (0.50 euros), *Zurban* (1.50 euros) and *Nova* provide an overview of what's on in Paris. Published every Wednesday.

CURRENCY CONVERTER

£	€	€	£
1	1.40	1	0.72
3	4.17	3	2.15
5	6.96	5	3.59
13	18.08	13	9.34
40	55.65	40	28.75
75	104	75	53.89
120	167	120	86
250	348	250	180
500	696	500	359

$	€	€	$
1	0.92	1	1.09
3	2.75	3	3.27
5	4.58	5	5.45
13	11.92	13	14.18
40	36.67	40	43.64
75	69	75	81.82
120	110	120	131
250	229	250	273
500	458	500	545

For current exchange rates see www.xe.com

USEFUL PHRASES FRENCH

IN BRIEF

Yes/No/Maybe	oui/non/peut-être
Please/Thank you	s'il vous plaît/merci
Good morning!/afternoon!/ evening!/night!	Bonjour!/Bonjour!/ Bonsoir!/Bonne nuit!
Hello!/goodbye!/See you!	Salut!/Au revoir!/Salut!
Excuse me, please	Pardon!
My name is...	Je m'appelle...
I'm from...	Je suis de...
May I ...?/ Pardon?	Puis-je ...?/Comment?
I would like to.../ have you got...?	Je voudrais .../ Avez-vous?
How much is...?	Combien coûte...?
I (don't) like this	Ça (ne) me plaît (pas).
good/bad/broken	bon/mauvais/cassé
too much/much/little	trop/beaucoup/peu
all/nothing	tout/rien
Help!/Attention!	Au secours/attention
police/fire brigade/ ambulance	police/pompiers/ ambulance
Could you please help me?	Est-ce que vous pourriez m'aider?
Do you speak English?	Parlez-vous anglais?
Do you understand?	Est-ce que vous comprenez?
Could you please ...? ...repeat that ...speak more slowly ...write that down	Pourriez vous ... s'il vous plait? répéter parler plus lentement l'écrire

DATE & TIME

Monday/Tuesday	lundi/mardi
Wednesday/Thursday	mercredi/jeudi
Friday/Saturday/ Sunday	vendredi/samedi/ dimanche
working day/holiday	jour ouvrable/jour férié
today/tomorrow/ yesterday	aujourd'hui /demain/ hier
hour/minute	heure/minute
day/night/week	jour/nuit/semaine
month/year	mois/année
What time is it?	Quelle heure est-t-il?

Tu parles français?

"Do you speak French?" This guide will help you to say the basic words and phrases in French.

It's three o'clock	Il est trois heures
It's half past three.	Il est trois heures et demi
a quarter to four	quatre heures moins le quart

TRAVEL

open/closed	ouvert/fermé
entrance/exit	entrée/sortie
departure/arrival	départ/arrivée
toilets/restrooms / ladies/gentlemen	toilettes/ femmes/hommes
(no) drinking water	eau (non) potable
Where is...?/Where are...?	Où est...?/Où sont...?
left/right	à gauche/à droite
straight ahead/back	tout droit/en arrière
close/far	près/loin
bus/tram/underground / taxi/cab	bus/tramway/métro/taxi
stop/cab stand	arrêt/station de taxi
parking lot/parking garage	parking
street map/map	plan de ville/carte routière
train station/harbour/ airport	gare/port/ aéroport
schedule/ticket	horaire/billet
single/return	aller simple/aller-retour
train/track/platform	train/voie/quai
I would like to rent... a car/a bicycle/ a boat	Je voudrais... louer. une voiture/un vélo/ un bateau
petrol/gas station	station d'essence
petrol/gas / diesel	essence/diesel
breakdown/repair shop	panne/garage

FOOD & DRINK

The menu, please	La carte, s'il vous plaît.
Could I please have ...?	Puis-je avoir ... s'il vous plaît
bottle/carafe/glass	bouteille/carafe/verre
knife/fork/spoon	couteau/fourchette/cuillère
salt/pepper/sugar	sel/poivre/sucre
vinegar/oil	vinaigre/huile
milk/cream/lemon	lait/crème/citron
cold/too salty/not cooked	froid/trop salé/pas cuit

with/without ice/sparkling	avec/sans glaçons/gaz
vegetarian	végétarien(ne)
May I have the bill, please	Je voudrais payer, s'il vous plaît
bill	addition

SHOPPING

pharmacy/chemist	pharmacie/droguerie
baker/market	boulangerie/marché
shopping centre	centre commercial
department store	grand magasin
100 grammes/1 kilo	cent grammes/un kilo
expensive/cheap/price	cher/bon marché/prix
more/less	plus/moins
organically grown	de l'agriculture biologique

ACCOMMODATION

I have booked a room	J'ai réservé une chambre
Do you have any ... left?	Avez-vous encore ...?
single room/double room	chambre simple/double
breakfast	petit déjeuner
half board/	demi-pension/
full board (American plan)	pension complète
shower/sit-down bath	douche/bain
balcony/terrace	balcon /terrasse
key/room card	clé/carte magnétique
luggage/suitcase/bag	bagages/valise/sac

BANKS, MONEY & CREDIT CARDS

bank/ATM/pin code	banque/guichet automatique/code
cash/credit card	comptant/carte de crédit
bill/coin	billet/monnaie

HEALTH

doctor/dentist/	médecin/dentiste/
paediatrician	pédiatre
hospital/emergency clinic	hôpital/urgences
fever/pain	fièvre/douleurs
diarrhoea/nausea	diarrhée/nausée
sunburn	coup de soleil
inflamed/injured	enflammé/blessé
plaster/bandage	pansement/bandage
ointment/pain reliever	pommade/analgésique

POST, TELECOMMUNICATIONS & MEDIA

stamp	timbre
lettre/postcard	lettre/carte postale
I need a landline	J'ai besoin d'une carte téléphonique
phone card	pour fixe.
I'm looking for a prepaid card for	Je cherche une recharge
my mobile	pour mon portable.
Where can I find internet access?	Où puis-je trouver un accès à internet?
dial/connection/engaged	composer/connection/occupé
socket/charger	prise électrique/chargeur
computer/battery/rechargeable	ordinateur/batterie/
battery	accumulateur
at sign (@)	arobase
internet address (URL)/	adresse internet/
e-mail address	mail
internet connection/wifi	accès internet/wi-fi
e-mail/file/print	mail/fichier/imprimer

LEISURE, SPORTS & BEACH

beach	plage
sunshade/lounger	parasol/transat
low tide/high tide/current	marée basse/marée haute/courant
cable car/chair lift	téléphérique/télésiège
(rescue) hut	refuge

NUMBERS

0	zéro	17	dix-sept
1	un, une	18	dix-huite
2	deux	19	dix-neuf
3	trois	20	vingt
4	quatre	30	trente
5	cinq	40	quarante
6	six	50	cinquante
7	sept	60	soixante
8	huit	70	soixante-dix
9	neuf	80	quatre-vingt
10	dix	90	quatre-vingt-dix
11	onze	100	cent
12	douze	200	deux cents
13	treize	1000	mille
14	quatorze		
15	quinze	½	un[e] demi[e]
16	seize	¼	un quart

STREET ATLAS

The green line indicates the Discovery Tour "Paris at a glance"
The blue line indicates the other Discovery Tours
All tours are also marked on the pull-out map

Photo: Notre-Dame

Exploring Paris

The map on the back cover shows how the area has been sub-divided

136

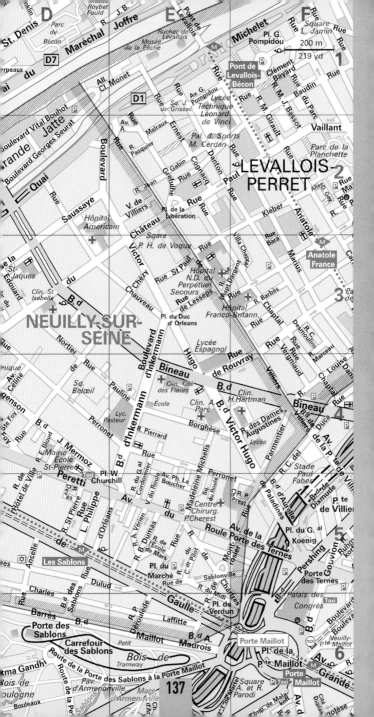
137

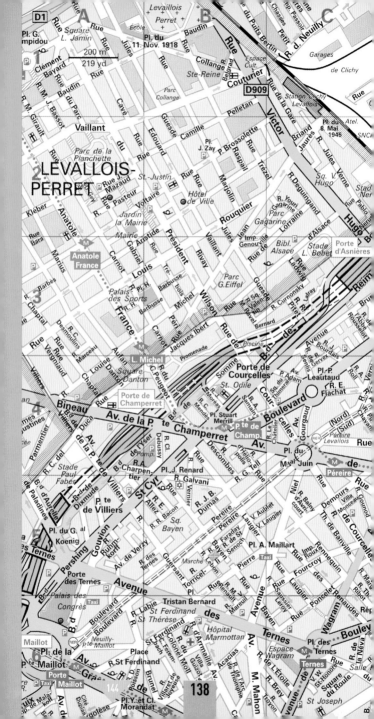

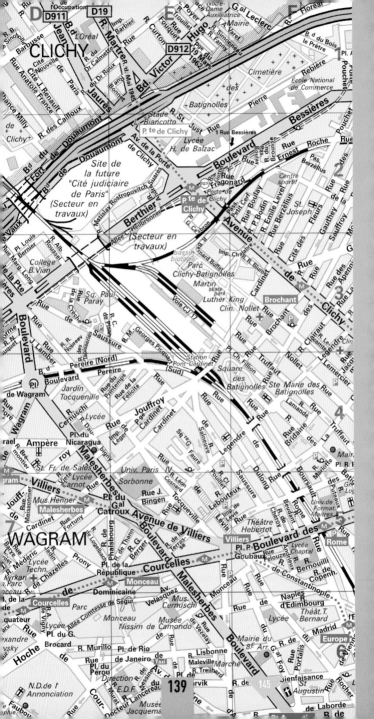

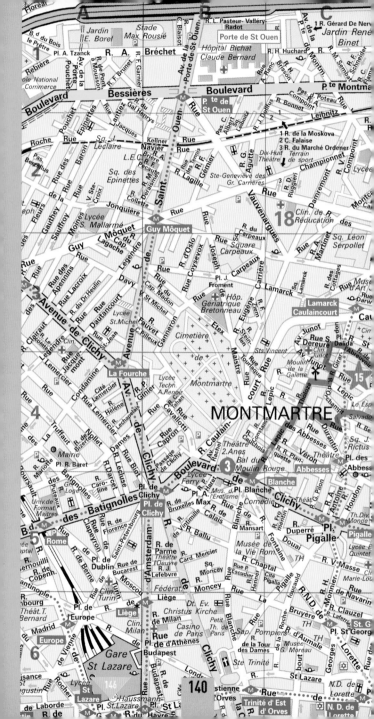

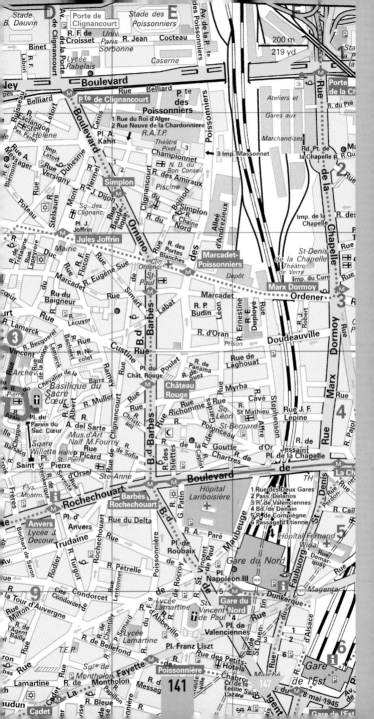

Labels visible on the map:

- Stade B. Dauvin
- Stade des Poissonniers
- Av. de la Pte des Poissonniers
- Porte de Clignancourt
- R. F. de Croisset
- Univ. Paris Sorbonne
- R. Jean Cocteau
- Caserne
- Binet
- Lycée Rabelais
- Av. de la Porte de Clignancourt
- 200 m / 219 yd
- BOULEVARD
- Rue Belliard
- P.te de Clignancourt
- Porte de la Ch...
- R. du Pré
- P.te des Poissonniers
- 1 Rue du Roi d'Alger
- 2 Rue Neuve de la Chardonniere
- R.A.T.P.
- Théâtre Pixel Championnet
- Ateliers et Gares aux Marchandises
- 3 Imp. Massonnet
- N.D. du Bon Conseil
- Rd. Pt. de la Chapelle
- Simplon
- R. des Amiraux
- Piscine
- Imp. de la Chapelle
- J. Dijon
- Sq. des Clignanc.
- Simplon
- E. Chaine
- Allée d'Andrezieux
- Pl. J. Joffrin
- Jules Joffrin
- Mairie
- R. des Portes Blanches
- Ornano
- Clig. Ordener
- St Paul
- Marcadet-Poissonniers
- Dépôt
- St-Denis de la Chapelle
- Théâtre de Verre
- Imp. du Cure
- Marx Dormoy
- Marcadet
- Ordener
- R. du Baigneur
- R.P. Budin
- R. Léon
- R.E. Duployé
- R.J. Robert
- Lamarck
- R. d'Oran
- Prison
- Doudeauville
- Custine
- Pl. du Chât. Rouge
- Poulet
- R. de Panama
- R. de Suez
- Rue de Laghouat
- Basilique du Sacré Cœur
- R. Muller
- Château Rouge
- R. Myrha
- Cavé
- St Mathieu
- Stephenson
- Rue J. F. Lépine
- Mus. d'Art Naïf M.Fourny
- Polonceau
- Sq. Léon
- St-Bernard
- Affre
- R. de Sofia
- R. des Islettes
- de la Goutte d'Or
- Pl. de la Chapelle
- La Ch...
- Boulevard
- Rochechouart
- Barbès Rochechouart
- Rue du Delta
- Hôpital Lariboisière
- 1 Rue des Deux Gares
- 2 Pass. Delanos
- 3 R. de Valenciennes
- 4 Bd de Denain
- 5 R de Compiègne
- 6 Passage d'Etienne
- Anvers
- Lycée J. Decour
- Trudaine
- Pl. de Roubaix
- R.A. Paré
- Hôpital Fernand Widal
- Gare du Nord
- Pl. Napoléon III
- Magenta
- Condorcet
- Lycée Lamartine
- St Vincent de Paul
- Gare du Nord
- Pl. de Valenciennes
- Dunkerque
- La Tour d'Auvergne
- R. de Bellefond
- T.E.P.
- Pl. Franz Liszt
- Rue des Petits-Hôtels
- Gare de l'Est
- Lamartine
- Sqe de Montholon
- Fayette
- Poissonnière
- Chabrol
- Cr. de la Ferme Saint Lazare
- 8 mai 1945
- Cadet
- R. Bleue

141

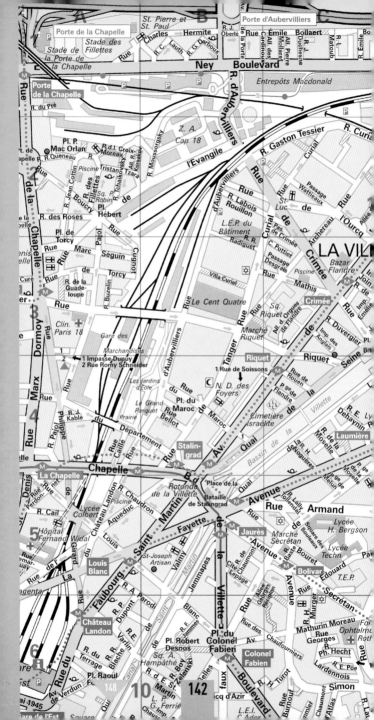

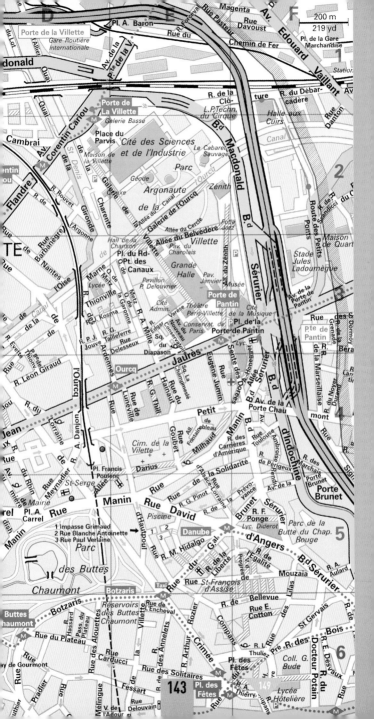

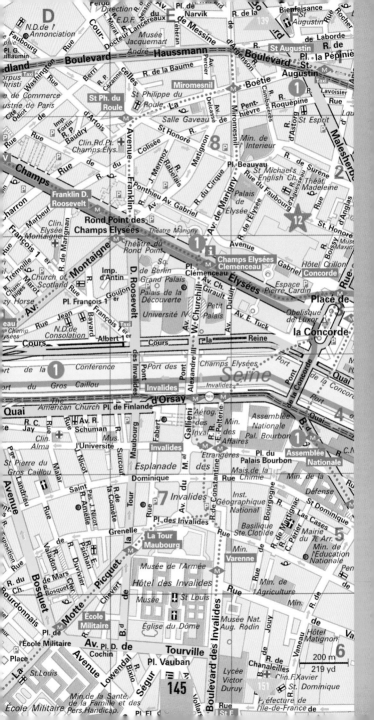

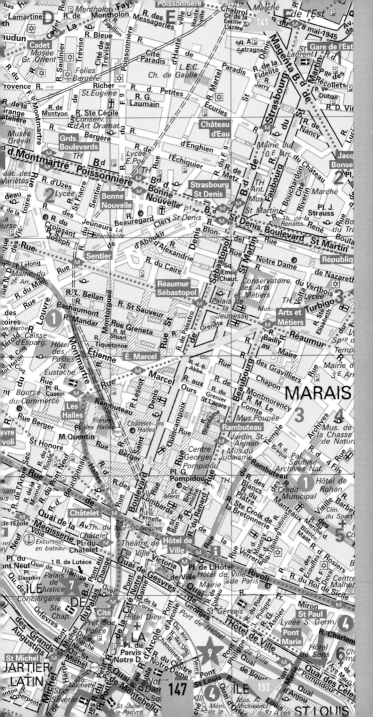

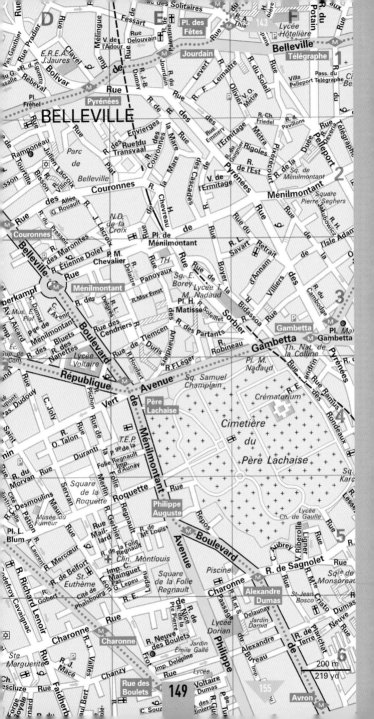

D E F

Rue des Solitaires
Pl. des Fêtes
R. A. Thie... 143
Lycée Hôtelière
Rue Fessart
Rue Mélingue
V. de l'Adour
Rue Delouvain
Belleville
Télégraphe
Jourdain
Villa Pelleport
Pass. du Télégraphe
R. du Soleil
V.O. Metra
R. F. Lemaitre
Olivier M...
R. de la
R. J.-B. Dumay
Rue du Jourdain
Levert
R. des
Rue Bolivar
Pl. Fréhel
Rue des
Rue de
Pyrénées
BELLEVILLE
R. de
R. Ch. Friedel
R. d. Pavillons
Rampeneau
Julien Lacroix
Parc de Belleville
R. des Envierges
Rue du Transvaal
Rue des Couronnes
Rue de l'Ermitage
Rigoles
R. de l'Est
Metra
Pixérécourt
Rue Télégraphe
Pelleport
Rue
Bisson
Villiers
Allée G. Rouault
Piat
Rue de la Mare
Rue des Cascades
Rue des Pyrénées
V. de l'Ermitage
Ménilmontant
Sq. de Ménilmontant
Square Pierre Seghers
Couronnes
des
R. J. Lacroix
N.D. de la Croix
H. Chevreau
Pl. de Ménilmontant
R. de l'Isle Adam
R. du Pressoir
R. des Maronites
Couronnes
Belleville
R. Etienne Dolet
P. M. Chevalier
R. Delaitre
Rue Panoyaux
TH
Rue de
Boyer
d'Annam
Viltiers
des
Rue des
Bluets
R. Max Ernst
Sg. E. Borey
Lycée T. la
M. Nadaud
Sorbier
R. du Cambodge
Ménilmontant
Boulevard
C. Avenir
R. L. Degras
Pl. H. Matisse
Soleillet
Bidassoa
Gambetta
Pl. Mar...
R. des Cendriers
R. des Partants
Gambetta
Pyrénées
R. des Nanettes
Rue de Tlemcen
Duris
Rue des Amandiers
Robineau
R. Robineau
Th. Nat. de la Colline
République
Plichon
Avenue
R.F. Léger
Gambetta
Pl. M. Nadaud
Dupont
Pas. Dudouy
C. Joly
Rue de la Roquette
Vert
de
Père Lachaise
Sq. Samuel Champlain
Crématorium
Cimetière du Père Lachaise
R. O. Talon
Rue Duranti
T.E.P.
Sq. de la Folie Regnault
Imp. d'Aunay
Ménilmontant
R. E...
Rondeaux
Morvan
Square de la Roquette
Merlin
Roquette
Rue
Repos
Sq. Karc...
Desmoulins
Musée du Fumeur
Servan
Rue Maillard
R. Gerbier
Philippe Auguste
Lycée Ch. de Gaulle
Pl. L. Blum
Mercœur
R. de Belfort
St. Euthème
Cité de Phalsbourg
Imp. C. Mainguet
G. Lepeu
R. de la Folie Regnault
Avenue
Boulevard
Aubrey
V. Riberolle
Rue de Sagnolet
Sq. de Monsoreau
R. Richard Lenoir
Chn. Montlouis
Square de la Folie Regnault
Piscine
Charonne
Alexandre Dumas
St-Jean Bosco
St-Cristo
Dumas
Godefroy Cavaignac
Gober
Rue
R. de Nice
R. Pierre
Passage
Delaunay
Jardin Damia
Neuve
Charonne
Rue
R. Neuve des Boulets
Lycée Dorian
Alexandre
Bureau
de
Panchai...
Ste Marguerite
R. J. Macé
Chanzy
Jardin Émile Gallé
Imp. Delpine
Lycée
Philippe
200 m
219 yd
esclure
Faidherbe
Rue des Boulets
149
Voltaire
Dumas
155
Avron

Gambetta
Belleville
Couronnes
Ménilmontant
Père Lachaise
Philippe Auguste
Alexandre Dumas
Charonne
Rue des Boulets

1 2 3 4 5 6

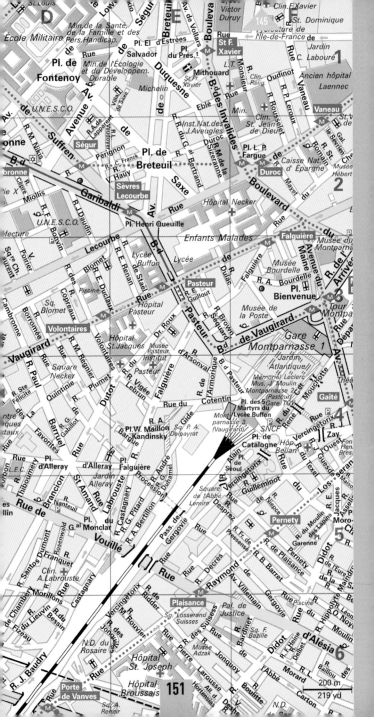

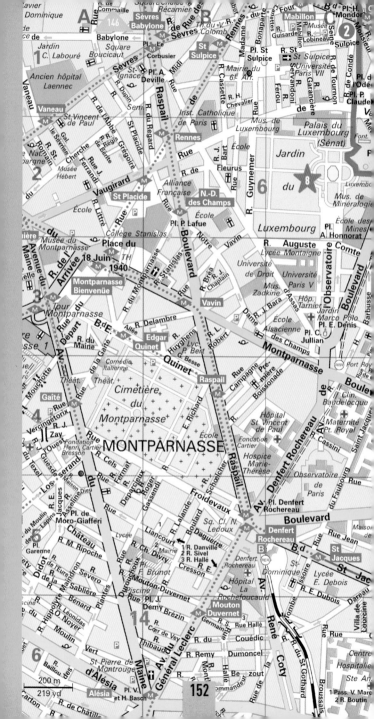

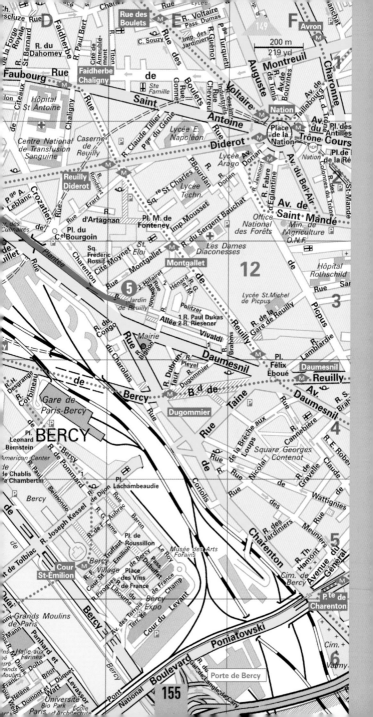

Les Arrondissements de Paris

A **B** **C**

1

LA GARENNE-COLOMBES

COURBEVOIE

ASNIÈRES-S-S

CLICHY

N 308

N 310

N 410

Porte St-O

Bd. de Verdun

Qu. du Prés. P. Doumer

Qu. du Maréchal Joffre

Seine

Bd. National

Quai Michelet

Quai d'Asnières

Bauron

Seine

N 309

Porte de Clichy

Barrière

Avenue

Bessières

2

La Défense

PUTEAUX

Boulevard Circulaire

Boulevard Circulaire

LEVALLOIS-PERRET

NEUILLY-S-SEINE

Porte de Champerret

Porte d'Asnières

Pereire

Batignolles

17

Bd. de Clichy

Rue de

Rue de Rome

Bd. de Batignolles

G St-I Haus

N 13

Ch. de Gaulle

Bd. M. Barrès

Bineau

Av. de Wagram

Av. du M. Gandhi

Longchamp

Palais des Congrès

Porte Maillot

Place

Av. de Friedland

Élysée 8

Palais de l'Élysée

Ste-Marie Madeleine

3

Bois

de

Boulogne

N 187

N 185

Porte Dauphine

Porte de la Muette

Av. Foch

Arc de Triomphe

Charles de Gaulle

Avenue des Champs-Élysées

Grand Palais

H

Petit Palais

Place de la Concorde

Obélisque

L

Av. Victor

Av. G. Mandel

Passy

16

Avenue P. Doumer

Palais de Chaillot

New York

Quai d'Orsay

Palais de Bourbon

7

Porte de Passy

Avenue

Tour Eiffel

Hôtel des Invalides

Maison de Radio France

Seine

Bd. Latour Maubourg

Av. de la Bourdonnais

Av. de Suffren

Av. de la Motte-Picquet

École Militaire

4

A 13

l'Hippodrome

Hippodrome d'Auteuil

Porte d'Auteuil

Porte de St-Cloud

Porte Molitor

Stade du Parc des Princes

Route de la Reine

N 307

Bd. Exelmans

Quai

Av. de Versailles

Citroën

Av. Émile Zola

Rue de la Convention

Rue Lecourbe

15

Vaugirard

Rue de Vaugirard

Gare Montparnasse

5

BOULOGNE-BILLANCOURT

N 10

Av. Ed. Vaillant

Bd. de la République

Quai d'Issy

Porte de Sèvres

Bd. Victor

Porte de Châtillon

Observa

Bd. Brune

6

MEUDON

CLAMART

Bois de Clamart

N 187

N 189

ISSY-LES-MOULINEAUX

Quai de Stalingrad

Av. du Verdun

Porte de la Plaine

VANVES

Porte Brancion

MALAKOFF

Porte de Vanves

Porte de Châtillon

Boulevard Gabriel Péri

N 306

CHÂTILLON

MONTROUGE

Porte d'Orléan

156

The index contains a selection of streets and places found in the street atlas

Autoroute / Autobahn		Motorway / Autosnelweg	
Route à quatre voies / Vierspurige Straße		Road with four lanes / Weg met vier rijstroken	
Route à grande circulation / Fernstraße		Trunk road / Weg voor interlokaal verkeer	
Route principale / Hauptstraße		Main road / Hoofdweg	
Autres routes / Sonstige Straßen		Other roads / Overige wegen	
Rue à sens unique / Einbahnstraße		One-way street / Straat met eenrichtingsverkeer	
Zone piétonne / Fußgängerzone		Pedestrian zone / Voetgangerszone	
Information - Parking / Information - Parkplatz		Information - Parking place / Informatie - Parkeerplaats	
Chemin de fer principal avec gare / Hauptbahn mit Bahnhof		Main railway with station / Belangrijke spoorweg met station	
Autre ligne / Sonstige Bahn		Other railway / Overige spoorweg	
Gare RER / RER-Bahnhof		RER Station / RER Station	
Métro / U-Bahn		Underground / Ondergrondse spoorweg	
Église remarquable - Autre église / Sehenswerte Kirche - Sonstige Kirche		Church of interest - Other church / Bezienswaardige kerk - Andere kerk	
Synagogue - Mosquée / Synagoge - Moschee		Synagogue - Mosque / Synagoge - Moskee	
Monument - Auberge de jeunesse / Denkmal - Jugendherberge		Monument - Youth hostel / Monument - Jeugdherberg	
Poste de police - Bureau de poste / Polizeistation - Postamt		Police station - Post office / Politiebureau - Postkantoor	
Hôpital - Bus d'aéroport / Krankenhaus - Flughafenbus		Hospital - Airport bus / Ziekenhuis - Vliegveldbus	
Zone bâtie, bâtiment public / Bebauung, öffentliches Gebäude		Built-up area, public building / Woongebied, openbaar gebouw	
Zone industrielle / Industriegelände		Industrial area / Industrieterrein	
Parc, bois - Cimetière / Park, Wald - Friedhof		Park, forest - Cemetery / Park, bos - Kerkhof	
MARCO POLO Tour d'aventure 1 / MARCO POLO Erlebnistour 1		MARCO POLO Discovery Tour 1 / MARCO POLO Avontuurlijke Route 1	
MARCO POLO Tours d'aventure / MARCO POLO Erlebnistouren		MARCO POLO Discovery Tours / MARCO POLO Avontuurlijke Routes	
MARCO POLO Highlight		MARCO POLO Highlight	

MARCO POLO TRAVEL GUIDES

The travel guides with **Insider Tips**

INDEX

This index lists all the sites and excursion destinations as well as important streets and squares referenced in the travel guide. Page numbers in bold type refer to the main entry listing.

WRITE TO US

e-mail: info@marcopologuides.co.uk

Did you have a great holiday?
Is there something on your mind?
Whatever it is, let us know!
Whether you want to praise, alert us
to errors or give us a personal tip –
MARCO POLO would be pleased to
hear from you.
We do everything we can to provide
the very latest information for your trip.

Nevertheless, despite all of our authors'
thorough research, errors can creep
in. MARCO POLO does not accept any
liability for this. Please contact us by
e-mail or post.

MARCO POLO Travel Publishing Ltd
Pinewood, Chineham Business Park
Crockford Lane, Chineham
Basingstoke, Hampshire RG24 8AL
United Kingdom

PICTURE CREDITS
Cover Photograph: Eiffel Tower/Flowers (Getty Images/Photographer's Choice: Ryan/Beyer)
Images: R. Freyer (8, 44, 60/61, 82/83, 84); Getty Images/Photographer's Choice: Ryan/Beyer (1); R. M. Gill (30, 78, 92/93, 98, 118, 118/119, 119, 122 top); huber-images: S. Bozzi (2/3), Cristofori (50), Damm (122 bottom), Gräfenhain (134/135), Kremer (36/37), S. Kremer (flap left, 52, 58/59, 111), H.-P. Merten (102/103); H. Krinitz (10, 47, 48, 55, 62, 114, 120, 120/121); Laif: Celentano (65), Galli (123), Henkelmann (7); Laif/hemis.fr (121, Escudero (66), Sonnet (4 bottom, 9, 72/73); Laif/RAPHO (89); Laif/Tripelon: Jarry (71); Look/age fotostock (12/13); mauritius images/age (17, 42, 46); mauritius images/Alamy (flap right, 4 top, 6, 11, 14/15, 18 top, 18 centre, 19 top, 19 bottom, 20/21, 22, 24/25, 26/27, 56, 70 right, 74, 77, 79, 81, 87, 91, 97, 101, 108, 117); mauritius images/imagebroker: J. Thomandl (18 bottom); mauritius images/Robert Harding (23); C. Naundorf (5, 32, 39, 40, 54, 69, 70 left, 94)

3rd edition – fully revised and updated 2016
Worldwide Distribution: Marco Polo Travel Publishing Ltd, Pinewood, Chineham Business Park,
Crockford Lane, Basingstoke, Hampshire RG24 8AL, United Kingdom. Email: sales@marcopolouk.com
© MAIRDUMONT GmbH & Co. KG, Ostfildern
Chief editor: Marion Zorn; Authors: Waltraud Pfister-Bläske, Gerhard Bläske; Editor: Arnd M Schuppius
Programme supervision: Tamara Hub, Ann-Katrin Kutzner, Nikolai Michaelis, Kristin Schimpf, Martin Silbermann
Picture editor: Gabriele Forst; What's hot: wunder media, Munich
Cartography street atlas: © MAIRDUMONT, Ostfildern; Hallwag Kümmerly+Frey AG, CH-Schönbühl/Bern; Cartography pull-out map: © MAIRDUMONT, Ostfildern
Design: milchhof: atelier, Berlin; Front cover, pull-out map cover, page 1: factor product munich; Discovery
Tours: Susan Chaaban, Dipl.-Des. (FH)
Translated from German by M. Abdelhady, Bonn; Jennifer Walcoff Neuheiser, Tübingen; editor of the English
edition: Christopher Wynne, Bad Tölz
Prepress: writehouse, Cologne; InterMedia, Ratingen
Phrase book in cooperation with Ernst Klett Sprachen GmbH, Stuttgart,
Editorial by Pons Wörterbücher

DOS & DON'TS ✋

A few things you should bear in mind in Paris

SEAT YOURSELF AT A RESTAURANT

When you go to a restaurant, don't make a beeline for the nearest table. In Paris it is customary to wait for a waiter to show you to your table. However, you may be able to change tables if the one initially chosen is not to your liking.

STAND ON THE LEFT SIDE OF AN ESCALATOR

The bigger the metropolis, the more frenzied the pace. If you stand on the left – the fast lane – of an escalator in one of the Métro stations or department stores, expect Parisians to give you a reproachful look.

WALK AROUND IN DANGEROUS NEIGHBOURHOODS

Most suburbs in the north, east and some southern areas of the city in particular are to be avoided. You should also be careful in the vicinity of the Strasbourg-St-Denis, Stalingrad and Châtelet-Les Halles Métro stations. The area around the Porte Dauphine and the Bois de Boulogne (street prostitution strips) likewise have a bad reputation.

DRINK BEER AT TOURIST TRAPS

If you crave a beer or two anywhere on the Champs-Elysées, Place du Tertre or near the majority of other tourist at-

tractions, you'll be in for a nasty surprise. The bill at such places can be steep, sometimes as much as three or four times higher than elsewhere. Also beware: a *démi* is not a half litre, but only 0.25 l.

FALL FOR THE "POOR TOURIST" SCAM

Be wary of people who lurk around the Eiffel Tower and the Arc de Triomphe claiming they are tourists who have had their credit cards stolen. They offer what they pass off as brand name clothing to unsuspecting tourists in return for money to help them get back home. Anyone who falls for this trap pays dearly.

EAT PIZZA

Although there are exceptions, the quality of pizza in Paris leaves a lot to be desired. Pizzas tend to be doughy, greasy and often lacking in proper ingredients. Only a few are baked in wood-fired ovens even though the prices are predictably high.

DRIVE IN THE CITY CENTRE

Paris is bogged down with traffic like no other major city. Apart from tourists attempting to get accustomed to the driving style in the city where the law of the jungle applies, massive traffic jams are also a bane for Parisians and a reality in their daily life.